THE CHALLENGE OF
TRUTH

The Reality of Being Human

SUSAN MUNIZ

Copyright © 2023 by Susan Muniz

All rights reserved. No part of this book may be reproduced or transmitted in any form or by any means, electronic or mechanical, including photocopying, recording, or by any information storage and retrieval system, without permission in writing from the publisher.

Published by Inicio Press
https://www.iniciopress.com/
The Challenge of Truth
Challengeoftruth.com

ISBN: 978-1-7380387-0-1
            978-1-7380387-1-8

"But such is the irresistible nature of truth, that all it asks, and all it wants, is the liberty of appearing."

—Thomas Paine

"During times of universal deceit, telling the truth is a revolutionary act."

—(Attributed to) George Orwell

I want to thank all that have offered me their time and encouragement in this effort. But especially want to acknowledge my husband for sharing his amazing journey with me. His perspective added greatly to my own understanding.

The Challenge of Truth © 2023—Susan Muniz

Contents

	Foreword	1
1	Preparing the Ground	3
2	The World is Your Classroom	7
3	Consciousness	11
4	Why Do We Lie?	17
5	The Consequences	21
6	Truth and Stress	27
7	The Clothing of Fear	31
8	Lifting the Veil	37
9	Need Versus Want	43
10	Expectation	47
11	Trust	53
12	Intent	57
13	What is True?	59
14	Belief and Awareness	63
15	Good Versus Bad	65
16	Truth and Prejudice	69
17	Community	75
18	Challenging Ourselves	77
19	Our Physical Nature	81
20	Signs and Symbols	85
21	To Act in Loving Ways	89
22	The Need for Connection	93
23	Truth and Relationships	97
24	Watch Out!	101
25	Blessing the Generations	107
26	The World Around Us	113
27	Empowerment	117

28	Thought and Prayer	121
29	Miracles	125
30	What is Spirituality?	129
31	How Truth Will Change You	133
32	The Spiritual Challenge	141
33	Turning on the Light	147

Foreword

Many years ago, I felt spiritually directed to write about truth and the challenge it presents to our lives. Composing this took decades. Even when I thought it was complete, I would set it aside and return to it much later, armed with fresh understanding. You see, it wasn't an answer to be found and forgotten or understood and defended but a deep dive into a personal revelation. I can't say even now that it is truly finished. It most likely never will be. Each revelation was not an end in itself but only a spark fueling my desire to understand more.

I trust that the ideas here have a purpose beyond me. At least, I hope that my efforts may prompt you to pause for a moment and consider things in new ways. Possibly be that spark for you. There is no intention here to threaten your beliefs or to convince you of mine. This simply offers a challenge for you to think about your thinking because we all should be more responsible and aware of how our choices impact those around us.

And as we see truth losing its societal importance, we become more likely to dismiss it as a personal value as well. But when truth loses its value, trust is lost as well. And trust is the necessary ingredient in all successful relationships, business or personal. So, agree or disagree with what is here or how I am portraying it, but you will see that the importance of truth is indisputable. So, spend a little time challenging what beliefs you cling to about yourself and the world. There is more to life than any of us realize, and the journey to find out what more there is does call to us.

Susan Muniz

1 Preparing the Ground

To plant a garden, you begin by breaking up the hard soil and removing the weeds. You create a clean, soft bed where the seeds you plant can take hold and grow. In reading this, you are the gardener, your heart and mind the compacted soil and truth the seed. Your willingness and attitude are the sunshine and water. The hardships you'll face are like the storms and droughts that are part of life. So, you are all of the parts of this planting and growing, and you will harvest an experience, weather its storms, and hopefully enjoy its fruit—fruits of understanding, health, better relationships, courage, all in all, a more fulfilling life. Your attitudes and intentions create your experiences. You can never be a passive participant in each moment because what you experience is a combination of *your* awareness and *your* reaction. So, harvest the moments that come because whatever understanding you glean will help you grow and make the next moments better.

"We cannot become what we want by remaining what we are."

—*Max De Pree*

The choice of how you react to the moment is yours, but the ramifications of your reaction ripple out to the world around you. Hopefully, the consequences you harvest are good ones.

> *"So, the servants of the household came and said unto him, Sir, didst not thou sow good seed in thy field?"*
>
> —Matthew 13:27

We usually think of growth as purely physical, but we can also grow and be healthy emotionally and spiritually. Inattention and neglect of yourself make you sick. You may try and remain physically fit but still lack any desire to be emotionally and spiritually fit. Just striving to feel safe, fed, and entertained as a life goal is a fragile existence. When we find that comfortable place in our homes, jobs, relationships, and faith, any change becomes the enemy. We steel ourselves against the storms in life, praying they don't take away what we have worked so hard to create. That fear of change hardens our hearts against learning and growing. When in fact, learning and growing are the basis for healthy change. Change doesn't happen to subvert your life but to grow it. Growing a better understanding of yourself is always beneficial. And the more you battle against change, the more you create the conditions for it. Change and hard times till and break up the hardened ground of your soul. And like winds and storms that strengthen the roots, we grow stronger when we are tested, and our faith deepens. Big change is scary, but you can begin by inviting easy changes into your life. Get involved in different activities. Be open to different ideas. Look deliberately at the thoughts and fears that make you want to defend yourself. And instead of running to avoid change, embrace the opportunity. Look at change as something positive. The adage, "When God closes a door, he opens a window," is very true. Look for the windows and other opening doors.

When young, our mental soil is soft and fertile, full of natural promise. Our heart and mind expand spiritually and intellectually as we spread our roots and make connections in the world. As with any fertile ground, the youthful mind takes it all in, weeds, fruits, and flowers. Learning and growing, reaching, and striving are everything. Even weeds aren't seen as weeds; all are beautiful and have purpose. There is no understanding of the moment being good or bad. A baby has no concept of lies. They believe everything. Filters and judgments are learned responses. A baby cries simply because they need. But their need is not attached to judgment. The emotional environment we are born into is the soil that grows us and informs our adult experience. To release ourselves from the subconscious landscape we have found ourselves in, we must recognize that is where we are; that is where the work will begin. We may have been raised in poor emotional soil, but we have the ability as adults to enrich it and work it in a better way.

The cycle of the seasons reflects our emotional lives. The spring signifies new life, growth, opportunity, and the promise of abundant understanding. Summer is when we nurture what we have planted. We have planted our curiosity; now, we can tend to our thoughts about our place in the world. Our thoughts begin to flower and bear understanding. In the autumn of us, we have the opportunity to mature in our reactions and responses. We can prepare for the emotional challenges ahead by taking ownership of our intentions and actions. Our emotional 'winters' will manifest as suffering and doubt. Doubt that will test our resolve whether to give power to those feelings or rise above them. As winter tests the standing nations of trees and plants breaking off the weakest parts, it can also be a period of rest. Harder times invite us to go within ourselves. Not necessarily to escape or excuse away our consequences but go within to find our strength and compassion. We can allow the strong winds to lash us but still remain secure in acceptance of what life brings. All the creatures of the earth know these cycles. All creatures know that seasons and hardships come and go. The willow knows that by bending to the wind, it will not break and that the bending isn't forever. The dead branches and debris cleared by winter ice and snow make new growth stronger in the spring. The fruits that are not harvested go back to the earth to make it fertile. No time or any changes that happen are useless.

> "In a way, Winter is the real Spring—the time when the inner things happen, the resurgence of nature."
>
> —Edna O'Brien

Unfortunately, our emotional "seasons" don't have the luxury of appearing at a set time on a calendar. We cannot always determine when we will need our strength or when our spring or winter will present itself, but the pattern of our personal seasons usually follows nature's plan. Dark times are usually followed by a spring, a hope. And our understanding and growth will be followed by a fall and winter, which will test us. You can't stop growing. To try and stop hurts. "Resistance is futile." And any form of sanctuary you may find will be fleeting at best. But the storms in our lives are important. Sometimes they come to clear your path.

> "There are some things you learn best in calm, and some in storm."
>
> —Willa Cather

Hard times may tell you where you need to heal or where you are the strongest. Our greatest gift is that each dawn brings us new chances and choices. But you've got to get a little dirty. But no one can do the internal work for you but you. Looking for answers outside of yourself and using someone else's mind can nurture your thoughts, but the answers must be your own before they can be the water and sunlight that grows you.

2 The World is Your Classroom

The world, the environment, society, your family, and your culture have formed you. But what you focus on and how you react teaches you as well. Let your experiences school you. You might ask, how did I act in that situation? Why did I react that way? If someone treated me harshly, what part did I play in their reaction? Did I act compassionately or out of fear? There are so many opportunities to get to know ourselves. The school of life has no semesters, requires no notes, but does test us. Your daily encounters are your classroom. There is nothing you can observe without it being a reflection of you. Whatever sense of peace and confidence you find is proof of the lessons you have learned.

The ability to understand is a gift, but the depth to which we understand the truth of something requires some extra effort on our part; we have to want to do it. The emotional and intellectual dances we do with one another are an important part of our schooling. Those mental "dances" involve looking at our expectations and intentions toward one another. Those interpersonal interactions are the best homework to uncover the truth about us. Our simple conversations give us an abundance of opportunities. Whenever we offer what is true of us, we trust it will be received in a good way, but in sharing, you are opening yourself to others' judgment or misunderstanding. Being that vulnerable will test your trust. But you can share without attaching your self-esteem to their reaction. Tell your story as a story and not as an opportunity to be correct or corrected. We should appreciate that others feel just as vulnerable when they share something personal. Remember the risk they are taking and reassure them and create a safe space. Learning to do that, learning how to be compassionate, refrain from judging, and share ourselves healthily are all high-level courses in this school.

Sitting or walking in solitude provides us with opportunities as well. Our classroom extends outside of the influence of others to the silence within us. Any time we spend alone, we get to think about thinking, get to think about why we are the way we are, but most importantly, we get to listen for answers or find better questions.

Plant your thoughts in each moment, each step, and watch where your steps lead you. All moments have been *pre-sent* to us. Perhaps even what we think of as chance is pre-determined and tailor-made to provide us with the opportunities each of us needs. We reflect our needs to the universe; how would it answer us other than with the moments we experience? Teachings come in all forms, but we only learn when we have the capacity to understand. Perhaps our teachers appear in human form or only as an experience. The realization that each moment has significance can seem overwhelming, but that proves how infinite the possibilities are. When you ask a question, the answers may be disguised in many different ways. You shouldn't disregard and prejudge an experience as unimportant just because it doesn't match your expectations. You mustn't assume you are the best judge of what you need and how that need should be met. The school of life is there to fulfill our purpose in the best way possible, and the lessons unfold over time and change as your perspective does. The same answer may have a different meaning at different times of your life. You may unknowingly be the teacher someone else is seeking. It doesn't matter that you do not have the answer, that you do not intend to teach, but arriving in that space at that time, you may give another what they need in their journey. That is what we do for one another. Your interactions with others aren't for you alone.

> *"Education is not the filling of a pail, but the lighting of a fire."*
> — *(Attributed to) William Butler Yeats*

Everything does happen for a reason. That may seem cruel considering the magnitude of the tragedies that come at times. But we are not being punished; events occur to move things on many levels. The consequence of them depends upon us. Consequences are always shared, both by the person causing the situation and by the person reacting to it. Everyone has made a choice that brings them to the moment, and the consequence of that choice has already been written in us. No one is immune to the storms that come; no one has a perfect blissful existence. But our struggles, no matter how difficult or lengthy, are always temporary. We can learn to be resilient and unshaken, with hearts not hardened and hiding but open and loving.

> *"When we meet real tragedy in life, we can react in two ways—either by losing hope and falling into self-destructive habits or by using the challenge to find our inner strength."*
> —*Dalai Lama*

Learning is as fundamental to our mental health as breathing is to our bodies. Many of us walk through life blind or deaf to the moment. Having the belief that our lives are just a matter of chance, fate, or luck, we give up thinking what we do will make a difference. Ignoring the moment, we are creatures of reaction, not response. When we treat what happens in our waking life as routine and unimportant the lessons that come to us go unrecognized. Unfortunately, it seems easier to believe in our dreams than to believe there is guidance all around us in our waking life.

"Wherever you are, be there totally."
—*Eckhart Tolle*

3 Consciousness

"Consciousness is the substance of life."
—*Joel Goldsmith*

Defined *according to Oxford Dictionary*
Subconscious: concerning the part of the mind of which one is not fully aware but which influences one's actions and feelings.
Consciousness: The state of being conscious; knowledge of one's own existence, condition, sensations, mental operations, acts, etc.
It is important to understand the concepts of subconscious versus conscious thought. You are surrounded every day with information, events, and behaviors that become part of your experience. We don't stop every time we experience something and think about it, but we do take it in. All we experience becomes a part of our subconscious and the fodder for our reactions. Our subconscious takes everything in and saves all those memories for future reference. But we can choose to be deliberate in our awareness and apply conscious thought to what we see and understand from a situation. When you don't act deliberately, you are adrift in the noise of the world; your behavior can be influenced without you realizing it. An obvious example is subliminal advertising. Advertisers count on you to make decisions based on brand recognition. Product familiarity is gained by constant exposure and repetitious messages that build a false trust in what product or idea is being sold. It is up to you to discern whether the product provides

what the advertising promised. By the time your money is spent, you seldom question your decision unless the results are disastrous; then, you may review your choice and how you made it. Subconscious acceptance of things as true can become deeply ingrained. Studies have proven that people tend to consider the first information they receive as true whether it is or not. And even when information is proven false, it is difficult for us to change our perspective. This is just as true for our perception of something advertised as it is for gossip or propaganda. It becomes hard to shake our first impressions.

"Any thought that is passed on to the subconscious often enough and convincingly enough is finally accepted."

—*Robert Collier*

You may not have the energy to thoroughly and thoughtfully engage in everything you hear each day. But you can be aware of the power of first impressions. Take a moment to consider where the information is coming from and what it seeks from you. Or where your judgment is coming from and what that tells you. It is interesting that when we hear information that agrees with our beliefs, even if those beliefs are fear-based or prejudicial, we never think to question them. But when a situation challenges what we believe, we are quick to see it as a threat and will be reluctant to believe it even if it is true.

Any time spent considering the truth of what surrounds us seems like another challenging burden we don't have time for. When we do have "free time," we'd rather spend it escaping life's daily routines, demands, and decisions that have piled up on us. All of the stuffing of our subconscious life. The behaviors you learned by example while growing up are a big part of your subconscious behavior.

But any of your ingrained routines or beliefs deserve some conscious thought.

One example is that many of us may have been brought up in families that use alcohol or drugs to escape stress. As children, we couldn't understand the mechanisms of adult behavior, so what we saw taught us that 'social drinking' is normal healthy behavior. We have been subconsciously conditioned to escape pain and responsibility whenever possible.

"Our subconscious minds have no sense of humor, play no jokes, and cannot tell the difference between reality and an imagined thought or image. What we continually think about eventually will manifest in our lives."

—*Sidney Madwed*

In time, if you desire to, you can begin to see when your subconscious drives the choices you make. You have the ability to understand what motivates you to behave in certain ways, and once you understand that you can make an empowered decision about it. Be an explorer of yourself; tap into what lies at the deepest part of your mind. Recognize and let go of what stands in your way, like unhealthy habits, reactions, and unreasonable fears. Identify the underlying needs that drive you or cause you to manipulate others. Question your old patterns and ways of coping. You may justify what you've been doing by believing that "it doesn't matter," or "I'm too old to change," or you "don't care." It's scary, especially later in life, to invite change. You've convinced yourself that the effort is too great, or worse yet, believe you deserve what has become of your life and your dreams. But that ship hasn't sailed; it still waits at the dock for you to captain it. It's never too late.

> *"Where is the Life we have lost in living? Where is the wisdom we have lost in knowledge? Where is the knowledge we have lost in information?"*
>
> —T.S. Eliot

So, what are easy ways to begin? Thinking consciously means bringing your mind to task and being well-informed before you decide something. That 'something' can be a decision or a feeling. There can be big financial or emotional decisions, often small decisions, and reactions. The best test of your control is when you are triggered by something and feel threatened. Take that moment to realize that your first tendency will be to react emotionally. So, the first decision to make is about how you will react. Will you let your flight/fight mechanism kick in, or will you consider other ways to respond? Does the circumstance make you defensive, angry, or just frightened? Can you place your awareness on what you are feeling and why rather than on the perceived threat? For example, you walk up to a fence, and suddenly, a large dog runs at you from the other side. That threat elicits a strong fear reaction in you. But you quickly determine that the dog is behind the fence and not an actual threat, so you choose not to run away. Running is a reaction; understanding the truth of the threat is a conscious response.

Think about all the things you believe and why. Is it just a subconscious acceptance of what others hold as true? Are there certain people that you subconsciously distrust because of their race or religion? Has anyone of that race done anything to you to warrant your distrust?

> *"The only path by which another person can upset you is through your own thought."*
>
> —Joseph Murphy

Conscious thought means *you* get to decide. And if truth matters to you, then you have to understand that your reaction to others is your responsibility. Give people a break from *your* beliefs and prejudices. Build some bridges of trust.

"A great many people think they are thinking when they are merely rearranging their prejudices."

—*William James*

Consciousness is life aware of itself. It is the living and breathing act that connects us to the world. It is the void that calls to be filled with understanding. Directed (conscious) thought forms our best intentions and creative drive. To be led solely by our subconscious can barely be called living. To ignore the present and only live through your past or for your future is ignoring what is real and true in the present moment. The past and future have no real form. There is only now. To act consciously is to look at what surrounds us right now and healthily interact with that reality.

"Until you make the unconscious conscious, it will direct your life, and you will call it fate."

—*C.G. Jung*

"Ego implies unawareness. Awareness and ego cannot co-exist."

—*Eckhart Tolle*

---

4 Why Do We Lie?

We lie to protect ourselves. We try and defend our actions because we are afraid of the consequences or are afraid of being judged. As young children, we learn to lie to hide our actions, avoid punishment or be seen as a failure, but most importantly, to protect ourselves from painful judgment. A young child in poverty may lie about their family's situation so they won't be teased or judged as worthless. The smallest child instinctually knows that lying is wrong and disrespectful. So even feeling that they must lie creates more shame about who they are. The world is cruel, and we don't equip children with the tools to deal with the complexities of human interaction. Anytime we feel we aren't enough as we are and are troubled about meeting others' expectations, it further erodes our self-esteem. We still react as children, feeling shame for who we are. We become content to lie and pretend. People also lie to conceal their manipulation of others. So, some of us lie out of fear, others out of a desire to control.

Whenever you lie to someone, you are taking away their ability to make a good choice because they don't have true information. If you lie to get what you want, you will never get what you actually spiritually need. The consequence of a lie may or may not show up on your doorstep immediately, where you can say, "Oh, there you are!" But it always shows up within us.

"Father, forgive them for they do not know what they are doing."

—Luke 23:34

When you lie about something, you'll expend a lot of mental effort defending the falsehood, constantly being on guard not to be discovered. We lie because we are afraid of being truthful, and then we are afraid of being found out. In trying to gain control of the consequences, we actually have lost control. But it bears repeating that no matter why we lie, make up excuses, or silently refrain from admitting the truth, we behave that way to defend ourselves from judgment. That doesn't mean we are weak or must accept any judgment as true (they seldom are). We just don't want to be judged. We don't want to defend ourselves or be challenged. But your harshest judge will always be yourself. Stop comparing yourself to who you believe others to be. Believing in someone's outer appearance is no less a judgment than what you resist from others. What you believe about someone else is not the truth of who they are any more than what others believe is true of you.

"We tell lies when we are afraid... afraid of what we don't know, afraid of what others will think, afraid of what will be found out about us. But every time we tell a lie, the thing that we fear grows stronger."

—*Tad Williams*

We all have a basic yearning to be understood and accepted, but then we make that understanding impossible when we hide what is true about us. For example, slowly and deliberately say to yourself, "I want to be clearly seen for who I am." Now watch how you feel when you say that. You may be surprised to discover your response may be a sort of mild panic, a slight rush of adrenaline. This is normal; that physical reaction is your fear of being seen and judged; your ego seeks to protect itself. This is the deep emotional reaction you will face whenever you try to tell the truth. This will happen even if you feel you have nothing to hide. Your mind is a very powerful instrument conditioned to protect itself from any threats to your self-concept, so you need to gently reframe and restrain that emotional reaction. Tell yourself not to be afraid; nothing bad is going to happen, and being seen is a good thing. Because whatever comes, no matter what, can be that good thing, a tool of change and growth. Find the gold!

"We swallow greedily any lie that flatters us, but we sip only little by little at a truth we find bitter."

—Denis Diderot

Truth can be bitter; most medicine is. But truth *is* medicine and will help heal you. Telling the truth can heal you physically, emotionally, and spiritually. The core of honesty and courage is being vulnerable and having honest interactions when it is hard, not just the easy parts. If you want to be understood, you have to allow that understanding to occur, even the parts of you that you are still unhappy with. Let go of lying to hide or gain; try something different. The parts of you that you feel the need to lie about are just the ones that need to see the light of day.

One thing to practice is to stop excusing yourself. Stop trying to defend your actions. Perhaps you are late, or you forgot something. No, the dog didn't eat your homework, and you were feeling fine when you said you were sick. Stop making yourself afraid and trying to find an "out." Pause for a moment and stand up and acknowledge what you have done. The poor decisions you try to excuse away are usually not such a big deal. We all make mistakes. Since your reactions always follow your intent, your anxiety lets you know when your intent is to be dishonest with someone, even before you act. Admitting the truth may be momentarily scary, but it will benefit you far more than your excuses will. Don't try to control others or control the situation; control yourself.

"No one can make you feel inferior without your consent."
—Eleanor Roosevelt

"A lie will easily get you out of a scrape, and yet, strangely and beautifully, rapture possesses you when you have taken the scrape and left out the lie."
—Charles Edward Montague

5 The Consequences

When we react to a situation, we may wonder what caused us to feel that way. Without some self-reflection, we are like a bull in a shop full of china, arbitrarily bashing around and then gingerly avoiding the broken glass. But it is not just the bull that can be injured by the broken glass, but anyone else coming into the shop afterward. Our unconsidered actions not only affect us but the lives of those around us. When we refuse responsibility and blame others when things don't go our way, we aren't thinking of them, only ourselves. Consequences come from any decision we make or action we take, even when we refuse to take any action at all. When consequences occur, we may see them as just good or bad luck. We seldom look back to see the origin or consider that if we did things differently, the outcome would be different as well. Under the philosophy that we reap what we sow, we are our own worse proprietors. We all "let loose" emotionally at times, in the intensity of the moment, without considering where the outburst will lead us or what the consequence will be. We may feel we have a right to express our emotions, but hopefully, once we regain our composure, we will look back at what drove us to act that way and make amends for what misunderstanding or hurt we may have caused. When we "own" our actions, we are at least able to recognize the consequence as something we have chosen and learn from it.

> *"Accountability feels like an attack when you're not ready to acknowledge how your behavior harms others."*
>
> —Steve Maraboli

> *"The cave you fear to enter holds the treasure that you seek."*
>
> —Joseph Campbell

Most programs for substance abuse include a requirement that you make amends to those you have injured by your behavior. Being willing to face the consequences and make amends to what degree you can may transform that hurt into a heartfelt connection. By sharing, you are inviting people in rather than pushing them away. And your intent to make things right is what grows you. Responsibility for your behavior doesn't just disappear because you ignore it. All the "lessons" that were given to you are still there waiting for your attention. When you finally accept responsibility, you will learn from them and hopefully make better, more compassionate decisions next time.

It can be very uncomfortable to weigh the effects of what you have done. You may deny you had anything to do with another's suffering or reason that you don't care what others feel or think. But feigning indifference is just another lie turned against yourself. What we do to others, we do to ourselves as well. It's hard to believe that if you knew the true effect of your behavior that you would still choose to do it. Even in cases where your behavior is simple thoughtlessness, your effect on another may be more than anyone should be expected to bear. We never know the weight each of us carries and what will constitute "too much." Shouldering some responsibility for another's suffering when you caused it is a very human obligation. The consequences demand it. Everything needs to find balance eventually. Some would describe it as getting closure. We won't easily forget what we left undone. It eats away at us. If we continue to act in ways that hurt others, we will constantly be on guard from being hurt, being judged. You may justify your actions, "I didn't have a choice," but there always is one. Don't let your choices deny someone theirs. Remember that your actions don't happen in a vacuum, and the consequences fall on us all.

"Nobody ever did, or ever will, escape the consequences of his choices."

—Alfred A. Montapert

So, *we* are the ones choosing our consequences; they are not judgments or punishments from God. Consequences are lessons we choose for ourselves every day. A friend once told me that he counsels his children about "life-changing" decisions. He tries to help them recognize that decisions about things like sex, drugs, alcohol, and other risky behaviors are ultimately life-changing ones that will follow them into maturity. When we are young, we don't realize the extent to which our choices follow us throughout our lives. Even as adults, how many decisions do we make daily without appreciating the consequences we created for ourselves? How often do we explain things away by blaming others or chalking it up to bad luck? But be aware that you will repeat some consequences over and over in your life until you transcend the need to experience them. You do that by changing the behavior that created them.

We usually think of consequences as something unpleasant, but there are consequences to the good that we do as well. A consequence of clear thinking and compassion can be health, wealth, and happiness. Love and joy are also born from our decisions and intentions. We create our future. What we put out to the world comes back to us many times over.

"Everybody, sooner or later, sits down to a banquet of consequences."

—Robert Stevenson

Be your own moral compass, listen to your inner voice and conscience, and let it guide you to what is best. If something doesn't feel right, don't do it. If it will hurt someone, don't do it. Remember the cartoons of the "good conscience" and "bad conscience"? The little angel and devil were sitting on opposite shoulders of a person whispering in his ear, trying to persuade the poor soul which direction to go. Unfortunately, we don't have a series of angels, like in the story *A Christmas Carol* letting us look at our life as it was and as it could be and awaken us in time to change it. The choices we make evolve into the lessons we need. A little self-reflection now and then will reward you with a life without significant regret. Reflect upon your feelings when they arise, put the brakes on your reactions, and ask yourself why you feel that way. Then decide how to respond or not to react at all. By responding in a better way, the consequence of that interaction will be growth and understanding. After a while, a better thought process will become second nature to you, and your response to the world will mature.

The native people of this country have a creed that everything you do should be done honoring the sacrifice of the past seven generations and for the benefit of the seven generations to come. That philosophy teaches us how to respond in the present. Remember that many of your decisions have consequences that may not be yours alone to shoulder but something your children and grandchildren will inherit.

"What you leave behind is not what is engraved in stone monuments, but what is woven into the lives of others."

—Pericles

"You and I are infinite choice-makers. In every moment of our existence, we are in that field of possibilities where we have access to an infinity of choices."

—*Deepak Chopra*

---

6   Truth and Stress

There is a tolerance level within each of us. A tipping point between remaining calm and feeling threatened in some way. That point can vary depending on how conditioned we have become to specific circumstances, people, and events. If a situation is unknown or if there is a great degree of similarity between the present moment and a prior threatening experience, we are more likely to experience our "buttons being pushed" and feel actual physical symptoms of fear, whether your reaction is a rational one or not. An increased pulse, flushing of the skin, increased respiration, all the fight-or-flight reactions are holdovers from the oldest part of our human experience. Even if the perceived threat simply challenges your understanding or belief, it will be the same physiological reaction. On a daily basis, we seldom worry about being attacked, but we are still using an ancient survival mechanism (flight, fight) in response to our modern anxieties. Those internalized fear reactions turn into chronic stress that threatens your health. Obviously, it's not easy to overcome those reactions when your past trauma is deep and central to your being. The key is to become more attuned to what triggers you by recognizing those physiological symptoms as they occur. Whenever you become uncomfortable, it is only natural to latch onto anything that gives you a feeling of security. You perceive something as a threat because it challenges you somehow, perhaps reminding you of a time you were hurt or confused. Or the situation may be something completely new, and being unknown is a challenge to you as well. If it challenges your beliefs, you will defend them. If it frightens you, you will try to hide, deny, or attack it. The circumstance may overwhelm you, but instead of controlling your feelings, you will try and control the situation by lying, making excuses, or even physically or intellectually defending yourself. But you have lost control of any action you take out of fear or anger. We want to be a victim of what is outside of us. We need to set up a threat we can defend against. Fear is the true enemy, the true threat to your security. You can overcome some fears not by fleeing or fighting but by remaining in control of your reactions. Don't give fear power over you. Don't blindly believe in what you are feeling. Give the moment a chance for the truth of it to reveal itself.

It is interesting to consider that even law enforcement personnel who receive intense training to de-escalate physical threats still tend to 'react' with overwhelming force to the threats they perceive. To control perceived threats, not necessarily to control their own reactions. But you aren't dealing with constant challenges to your safety; there is usually time to control your reactions by simply being honest about how you are feeling and why. The minute you are "triggered," you can admit that you are. Allow yourself to feel it but not fight it. Don't look to attach that feeling to someplace or someone, which will just create another trigger.

"Those who make conversations impossible, make escalation inevitable."

—*Stefan Molyneux*

If you continue to resurrect your memories to define new experiences, your reactions will always be related to that memory rather than the current circumstance. Thinking about things in a new way creates a new "memory" that can change your future reactions. What happened in the past may have been true, but that is not this moment. Don't focus only on what you believe is making you feel that way. Don't run from it or cover it up or hide behind excuses; that only reinforces the fear you felt before. No matter how much you practice conscious living or how honest and real you are with yourself, your subconscious memories will always be a part of you. Some memories may remain hidden until you try to make sense of something and are suddenly thrown into a panic. Some conditioned responses from the past will cause you to put up a defense and your heart to race as you process the best way out. Let those triggers be your catalyst to change. Allowing yourself to feel honestly doesn't mean you will experience that same feeling forever. If you can step outside yourself for a moment, you'll see that the fear and stress of a situation will pass and usually passes pretty quickly.

> *"The greatest weapon against stress is our ability to choose one thought over another."*
>
> —*William James*

When you look under the bed, you'll see the bogeyman isn't really there. You can disassociate yourself from your gut reaction and transmute any feelings into loving ones.

> *"Your triggers are pathways to your wound. The stimulus is only a door."*
>
> —*Sanhita Baruah*

7 The Clothing of Fear

We dress ourselves in many ways for many reasons. Primarily to protect ourselves from the elements but also as a form of self-expression. What you choose to wear is who you want to be seen as or what makes you comfortable. When you feel fear, it makes you feel vulnerable, naked to the circumstance. To protect yourself from that, you cover it up with excuses, direct blame, or dress the fear up as whatever has triggered you and don't see it as a part of you any longer. You put the feeling off on others and believe that if you get away from or attack what you are fearful of, that fear will go away. But fear travels with us. It is part of who we are. It is part of our nakedness. We are able to change our attire any time we choose and easily dress for the part we want to play. It is the same in a way when we feel fear; the part we want to play is that it isn't us; it is what is outside of us. It is our choice how to feel about something or someone. Others don't have the power to decide how we feel. We have given that power to our memories. And in dressing up our fear, we choose what parts of us we show and which we hide.

"Most of us are ashamed of shabby clothes and shoddy furniture, let us be more ashamed of shabby ideas and shoddy philosophies…"

—Albert Einstein

I bring up our chameleon-like qualities because the same concept can be applied to our insecurities. We routinely cover up how we truly feel inside by focusing instead on how others see us. We dress up our insecurities with lies and our fear with blame and anger; we even dress up our lack of control by bullying others.

Fear is the strongest motivator of action and reaction. At its most basic, when we are afraid, it is because we are unable to control the unknown that surrounds us. But we can control what is within us. We do have control over ourselves. Even in thinking that we can defeat our fears, we are actually giving them power, power to be something we have to defeat, instead of just not giving in to those forms and feelings we have created. Don't try and get control over what you are reacting to but rather control how you are reacting. Instead of placing the focus of our feeling on what we believe triggered it, whether that is a situation or a person, we should choose to look at what is inside of us that makes us believe we are unsafe or insecure. Fear is a mental experience that triggers a physical reaction. It impacts our thinking and leaves us susceptible to reacting impulsively. When our fear leads to anger, stress, judgment, or acts of violence, all those things are an attempt to get control. We clothe our fear with those behaviors. So, if you put on your 'angry coat,' know you can take it off just as easily by recognizing you are just scared and defending yourself. We can never truly control what surrounds us. The world will always insert itself into our lives, and not always in pleasant ways. So, expect the unexpected. But rather than hiding, being angry, or placing the blame on your feelings, learn to control how you react to situations and look for the solution within you.

"Hide in the mirror. No one will look for you there."

—*Ljupka Cvetanova*

"...so, fear itself is even more corrosive, even more destructive than all the frightening potential of the thing that arouses it."

—Joe Henry

Fear abounds. We project fear onto the world around us anytime we are challenged. Challenged by our past experiences influencing the present moment, challenged anytime our beliefs are questioned or cause us to doubt or judge ourselves. We even have fears programmed into us by constant exposure to political speech and hatemongering. And the moment we allow a belief to find a home in us, it takes root and begins to define us. Not only is it scary to question what we have come to accept, but to trade a belief for deeper understanding is a challenge not many are willing to face. But it is a challenge that frees you. Understanding heals. Stop objectifying your fear. Fear is a feeling, not a person. It has always been easier to see our fears in the context of what triggered us because it gives us something or someone to run from or attack and another vivid memory to add to our "bank" of triggers. One stunning example we can all relate to is road rage, where someone's cumulative stress is projected out violently and indiscriminately on anyone that provides a convenient target for their anger and fear. In causing anger and fear in others around them, they only escalate the threat and create further fear.

There always is a momentary rush of adrenaline when confronted by the unknown. But you can try and reframe the feeling of fear as excitement! Treat it as if you have chosen that circumstance and expect it to be something good rather than something to fear, as if you are vacationing away from home and gladly seeking out new experiences. Experiences that may challenge you, but in the scenario of a vacation, you know you will always go back home, back to safety, so you choose to experience things even if they frighten you.

It is evident that at this point in our evolution, humans rely more on our intelligence than our physical prowess to survive. As our external monsters have been conquered (we no longer need to fear being eaten or attacked), our survival responses have shifted from defending ourselves against physical threats to defending our emotional security. Perhaps that is the scariest threat because we feel so defenseless on the inside. Just the idea that we should bring the battle to our understanding seems impossible. But it only takes a moment when you are challenged to decide whether your reaction is valid or imagined. If imagined, forgive yourself for believing that way and take pride in your effort to be stronger, more compassionate, and in control. You will begin to know that self-control will be the strongest source of your security.

In that security, we can be naked to the world. We don't have to armor our fears. It is incredible how much we hide emotionally and how exposed we always feel. It's sad just how much we deny ourselves and how many experiences are rejected. Just having the ability to excuse our choices comforts us! We have fallen in love with the immediate hiding place having an excuse gives us. We excuse our way out of admitting what we say and do and would like to believe it also excuses the consequences. We would rather live with a lie for years than with a consequence that may last only a moment. The greater the threat to our self-image, the greater the chance we will deny it is any threat to us.

"We only see what we want to see; we only hear what we want to hear. Our belief system is just a mirror that only shows us what we believe."

—Don Miguel Ruiz

And as the fable goes, even though the reality is that the emperor has no clothes on, he believes he is seen in fine robes.

> *"I couldn't stand living in a society that admires the emperor's new clothes, when I see so clearly that he is naked."*
>
> —Patricia McConnell

So be aware that when you are faced with anything new, whether that is an idea, person, or situation, you will run it through your "program" to determine how to react. That program is the culmination of your memories and experiences; we use it to inform how we should feel about any new experience. That all happens in a fraction of a second. But it is what we do next that defines us. Know that memories may help recall a threat from before, but that isn't now. New situations and ideas don't have to be a threat. Being new doesn't make it bad.

> *"Hate is a consequence of fear; we fear something before we hate it...."*
>
> —Cyril Connolly

You can think consciously and strive to accept things that may be new to you. In reality, the moments you experience will seldom be a true physical threat; more than likely it will be emotional. Either way, there is always something there for you to learn. Either way, isn't it worth taking just another moment of your time to think clearly?

"Fear keeps us focused on the past or worried about the future. If we can acknowledge our fear, we can realize that right now we are okay. Right now, today, we are still alive, and our bodies are working marvelously. Our eyes can still see the beautiful sky. Our ears can still hear the voices of our loved ones."

—Thich Nhat Hanh

8 Lifting the Veil

Over our lives, our subconscious experiences have created layers of belief that inform how we react to one another and define ourselves. But sadly, those beliefs and understandings become set in stone for many of us. Unmovable, not open for discussion. No room for doubt. We keep adding layer after layer of thinking that only reinforces it. But what if things aren't the way we believe them to be? What if the understanding we are so fixated on serves no need in a spiritual sense? Could you accept that what you have been taught to believe won't take you where you want to go? The truth that has been buried beneath our beliefs? As we get older, we naturally gain some perspective on the consequences and choices that have made up our lives. Perhaps you wish there was more to it than what you were led to believe. But all the experiences you have gone through can be seen and understood in a different way. Questions arise that don't seem to have answers. You doubt your ability to understand but don't dare doubt your beliefs. Beliefs are an important part of our spiritual nature, but when they create just another veil over the truth, it stops us from searching, although our spirit is still yearning, still unfulfilled. Think of a series of veils. One veil over you, you can still see pretty well. Two, you can still see, but things get fuzzy. Three or more, light may shine through, but your vision is blocked. Most of us only believe in what we can still see. We accept what the world tells us about ourselves and believe it. We believe it to our detriment. We are happy when people compliment us and depressed when we are criticized. We allow our identities to be woven by all the people that don't know us instead of getting to know ourselves by taking to heart what lies within us. We need to believe in ourselves.

The basis of your fears and beliefs began a long time ago, and you've invested a lot of time in defending or denying them. You have made a home for yourself there, so it will be scary to let them fall away. Your habits and beliefs have been your closest friends, but they could be lying to you. You want to believe in your friends that they always have your best interests in mind. But just like your fears will always be a part of you, your beliefs will be as well, but you can choose to understand them differently. You use your memories to protect yourself. Use your habits to hide you. Your belief to shelter you. The memory of something can be painful, but that experience and the pain you felt didn't protect you then, and it doesn't protect you now; it victimizes you. Sharing the intimate details of our pain helps us release it. We all need to feel heard and understood. But we also need to move on from our personal tragedies; they may describe the past, but they don't have to define us.

There is always immense peer pressure to be led by others and seek their approval, and we try to change and adapt to achieve that. But what do you gain? If you accept how others define you, you deny who you are. And they will see in you what they need you to be for them. Trying to be that for someone will only leave you feeling inadequate. Most of us accept that emotional environment even if it hurts us. Even when you know someone's picture of you isn't true, you will still try to be that. But you can paint a true self-portrait by sharing what *is* true for you. Know that your experiences *are* important and worthwhile and tell your story. Don't wait for others' permission to feel good about what you've been through or how you have handled something. You don't need their approval. Who you are is special; there is only one you. Lifting the veils (fears, beliefs, and self-judgment) that don't serve you anymore frees you from what has blurred your vision and self-concept. We are all battling our own demons and deserve each other's compassion, not judgment. For in judging others, we are attempting to define ourselves in relation to what we believe them to be.

> *"If you are willing to look at another person's behavior toward you as a reflection of the state of their relationship with themselves rather than a statement about your value as a person, then you will, over a period of time cease to react at all."*
>
> —Yogi Bhajan

As we walk through life, we make choices all day long that move us closer or push us further from the understanding we seek. Do you want to understand or become further entangled in consequence?

> *"When you choose an action, you choose the consequences of that action."*
>
> —Lois McMaster Bujold

The concept of understanding ourselves may be ridiculous to some. They may not even feel there is any value in self-reflection. We can remain more firmly entrenched in our beliefs or open ourselves to the opportunities before us. You can use the same peer pressure you have experienced, and reverse it, draw others into an effort to understand themselves by providing peer pressure of your own. Ask them to share and be real about themselves. Be a role model. You can begin your journey by striving to know the 'truth' of things, not necessarily scientific truth, but simply the truth of what you are experiencing, without the bias of your beliefs. But to start, you must know how you are biased and what that bias does to your interactions. Then identify what you are feeling and why you are feeling that way.

*"I chose to live by choice, not by chance;
To make changes, not excuses;
To be motivated, not manipulated;
To be useful, not used;
To excel, not compete.
I choose self-esteem, not self-pity.
I choose to listen to my inner voice, not to the random opinions of others.
I choose to be me."*

—*Miranda Marrott*

"Love and compassion are necessities, not luxuries. Without them, humanity cannot survive."

—*Dalai Lama XIV*

All of us want to believe in a proverbial "Great and Powerful Oz" or a knight in shining armor versus the quiet, insecure man behind the curtain. In the story, *The Wonderful Wizard of Oz* by L. Frank Baum, the visible manifestation of the Great and Powerful Oz was created to hide the simple truth of its creator's humanness and frailty. That great and scary Wizard was an embodiment of externalizing our fears by wearing the protective armor of lies. Accepting the little man behind the curtain means you must accept the responsibility of returning home alone. Dorothy, lost and meek in a strange land, would not have believed she always had the power to return home had she not gone through the trials she did. As the Great Oz ruled with fear, he pushed Dorothy and her friends to go on a journey, not expecting them to return. But they did return emboldened by the truth of themselves. When confronted with their truth, the Wizard was compelled to recognize the truth of them and himself. Our fears and consequences take us on a journey, but thankfully the same parable holds true; we each carry our home and security within us, and the love we are looking for and deserve is waiting for us to wake up. So, pull back the curtains and see the small, meek man that is your fear!

"You had the power all along, my dear."
   —*L. Frank Baum, The Wonderful Wizard of Oz*

---

9 Need Versus Want

Many of us stumble through life, feeling on top of the world when things go our way and despairing when they don't. We don't even get one desire satisfied before chasing after another. For many of us, there is never enough. But wanting only succeeds in perpetuating our sense of lack. We have convinced ourselves that having a new car or new shoes are needs. But we weren't put here to own a new car. You don't *need* to define yourself over and over by what you own or wear. You will never be truly fulfilled by the things you accumulate, and they will never adequately define you. Yes, you may *want* those "bright and shiny" things, but the thrill is fleeting, and those goods quickly lose their importance to us once attained. It is always about the next thing. Perhaps the drive to accumulate more is an internal symbol of spiritual and emotional yearning that has gone unfulfilled.

"Any so-called material thing that you want is merely a symbol: you want it not for itself, but because it will content your spirit for the moment."

—*Mark Twain*

Our truest needs are the ones we were born into this life with, the need for food, shelter, and love (security). There should be some contentment when our bellies are full; we have a roof over our heads and have some experience of love. But somehow, there still is this insatiable yearning that we keep trying to quench with a constant acquisition of material possessions. Even knowing that "you can't take it with you," we define our success according to what we have or can buy. Wanting is formed by comparing what others have versus what you don't. *Want* is egotistical and will never provide fulfillment, whereas *need* is from the heart.

"What I want is what I've not got. But what I need is all around me."

—Dave Matthews

Need is related to our truth. The truth of what you need physically, emotionally, and spiritually. You may not even be aware of your needs. But the desire to fulfill those needs seems hard-wired into our human experience. We yearn to be guided to what will fulfill us. Like the primal need to fulfill our sexual drive, the drive to understand is just as natural and compelling.

The word *want* is used so idly; we don't even consider that we are defining ourselves as "without," impoverished, suffering, in want. We routinely apply our desires and sense of deserving as a normal pattern of living. There is a Native American saying: "When you want, you cause the children to cry." Want is selfish, grasping, and inconsiderate. In wanting, you are not being grateful for what you have or caring about the needs of others. Want is jealous and inconsiderate. To want is to deny the needs of others. Want causes suffering in the midst of plenty and will never be satisfied. It is akin to eating jellybeans when we are starving. Candy is shiny and sweet but not nutritious, leaving us hungry with only a sugary rush that we must constantly satisfy.

But our wants aside; we are all needy. If not physically needy, then spiritually and emotionally so. Perhaps we are fortunate enough to be fed, healthy, and warm, but we inherently know there is more to us than the creature comforts we strive for. That sense of lack drives the decisions we make. But we think what we *want* will fulfill it, but it doesn't. Realize the difference between need and want before you chase after something. Look intently at all the obvious and complex consequences of getting what you want and then think consciously about those desires. Know the reality of what you will gain and whether that will ultimately improve your life. Think truthfully about your desires. *Wanting* puts distance between us, whereas fulfilling *need* connects us. Sometimes we recognize desire in ourselves and decide to give in to it, even knowing full well it won't truly satisfy us. But we can begin to take away the power of our satisfaction by realizing its transience. Let it satisfy the current moment, but don't expect it to satisfy the future.

When you consciously participate in your decisions, you should include the cost of consequences. There is always a risk whenever that cost is ignored. A simple example we can all relate to is when we imagine how wonderful it will feel to purchase a new car. And that desire overwhelms the practical consideration of how it will put us into debt and how that debt will add to our stress and insecurity. So, when making informed choices, you should try and factor in a future with those consequences, not a fantasy. All we have that *is* real is just the present moment. Your need is in that moment, so balance your wants against that. Want is fulfilled in the future, but the feeling is quickly delegated to the past. Therein is the beauty of truth; it is always present and will always beneficially guide you to fulfilling your true need. Truth is influential because it is the core of each second of your experience. So, know what *is* true and base your decisions on that, not what you 'want' to be true.

"It is easy to dodge our responsibilities, but we cannot dodge the consequences of dodging our responsibilities."

—*Josiah Stamp*

"Any story created about this moment is merely a confusion of the conceptual mind."

—*Eckhart Tolle*

10   Expectation

> *"Anger always comes from frustrated expectations."*
> —Elliott Larson

Expectation is an invisible action, a mental willing away of what another has or can provide without their consent.

Expectation is a secret projection of your needs and desires on others. Sometimes you may be counting on someone to do for you what you can't or won't do for yourself. Expectation is also part of a general sense of entitlement where we burden others with the responsibility to serve us. There are obvious expectations around gender roles and stereotypes in relationships, the workplace, or on the street. We carry around a basic construct of what someone should be able to do or be to us based on gender, nationality, age, color, or social class. When others fail to provide for us or don't do what we expect, we get angry and feel betrayed. Our understanding proved to be false. We feel lied to, even disrespected, by the person we made responsible. But remember, expectations usually aren't communicated or agreed on, especially in personal relationships, yet we still carry some belief that our partner should know what we expect. Having expectations guarantees you will live with resentment because others will always fail you. You have never given them a chance or a choice.

> *"Expectation is the root of all heartache."*
> —William Shakespeare

As a society, we regularly make contracts to make our expectations legally binding and to ensure the other party is aware of and committed to the agreement. Legal marriages are civil contracts, but other than to have and to hold through sickness and health; it doesn't really come close to enumerating the expectations we may have of one another. But obviously, the most damaging expectations are the invisible ones where we hold onto the assumption that the other person should know what we are expecting from them. Even when the expectation is to be loved, the many ways love can be expressed are open to interpretation. Unless our feelings are communicated, our expectations make us thieves of the other's intent and free will. And compounding that is the fact that expectations change; we just seem to make them up as we go along. And when some situation is uncomfortable for us, we shift the responsibility to others to take it on for us.

As a society, we have set up behavioral expectations in the form of stereotypes that we force upon others and ourselves as well. Society's expectations, like personal ones, set us up for failure. Stereotypes about what women can or can't do. What men should be. Who should be the "breadwinner"? Who should care for the children? The list would go on and on. But expectations at their most dangerous are the ones that evolve from our prejudices. Because when stereotypes feed prejudice, it is to legitimize our fear, and justifies our behavior toward each other.

Expectations can be good when we direct them to ourselves. Goals are a form of expectation that puts us in charge of our self-image. But we can only do that for ourselves; others can't expect others to achieve them. There is no compassion or love in expectation. We want to be able to depend on one another and feel supported, but that can only happen if we let one another know what we need. Some people even set up an expectation that they will be mistreated and then set the stage to prove themselves right. They see what they want to see in others' behavior. "I expected this; I knew it would happen; I'm not good enough." Many times, we base our personal and professional relationships on a fantasy. We blindly hope for what we want to be true, then make others responsible when it fails.

You may not be consciously aware of another's expectations, but you will subconsciously sense them and defend yourself. Your defense will be a subconscious one as well. All this invisible back and forth is guiding our lives! Generally, the reaction to being the object of others' expectations is to pull away and detach emotionally. You will stop believing in the fantasy. In a simple example, when someone grabs at you, you pull away; you don't have to think about it. That will naturally be the same reaction. Particularly when unvoiced, expectations actually will push others away as if you physically attacked them. Everyone subconsciously defends themselves from unspoken demands. We are all protective of our space and time. Obviously, this can create a lot of stress and dissatisfaction in the workplace where the expectations placed on workers (or on management by those they hire) are at odds with the workers' willingness and expertise to accomplish them. But also, in personal relationships where unmet 'needs or expectations from both parties go unfulfilled and eventually damage what might otherwise be a healthy relationship.

If you are wakeful and conscious, you can feel your anxiety increase due to someone's expectations, but perhaps you can't identify why; you cannot find the threat. But expectations are a threat. Because if they are not met, someone is placing the blame on you for their disappointment. You may begin to feel that person's resentment when you are around them, and consequently, will be more reluctant to do things for them (you will pull away). But it goes both ways; as you place expectations on someone else, you will also feel fear and anxiety because it is a deception, and you don't want to be caught in it. But most of us don't consciously decide to expect things from others; we just feel reliant on gaining the help we need from those we are close to. We hope our needs magically will be understood as we are reluctant to ask. Sometime when you are ready, and before irreparable harm occurs, you should have those vulnerable, intimate conversations and uncover the expectations that are coming between you. Clear the air. Bringing expectations into the open compassionately becomes a sharing, an opportunity to understand one another better. And once a need is known, whether or not it is met, it is at least no longer hidden or misunderstood.

Consider all the expectations you send out into the world. All the silent pulling and grasping with everyone competing for their wants and needs and all the avoidance and frustration that comes with it. A very obvious case is between parents and teenagers, where adult expectations drive their children's rebellious behaviors. Expectations that may be considered reasonable but will be seen as a threat to their sense of independence unless understood and agreed upon.

Expectations can destroy relationships. It is the push and pull of intimacy. The more you expect, the further you will push that person away. The more freedom and respect you give that person, the closer you will become. Giving another freedom to be themselves, to offer themselves without your expectation, actually attracts them to you.

"Never idealize others. They will never live up to your expectations. Don't over-analyze your relationships. Stop playing games. A growing relationship can only be nurtured by genuineness."

—*Leo F. Buscaglia*

Try letting go of your expectations for a day or two; you will quickly see the difference. Do that today, right now, and perhaps you'll see the results tomorrow. If you have needs, ask for help in a humble, non-expectant way, and generally, if they are able, others will be there for you. One way to avoid expectations is to acknowledge what others do for you without being asked. They will feel understood, and you will gain some gratitude. If your partner turns on your morning coffee, washes your clothes, or makes you dinner, don't think, "Well, that's their job" (that reflects your expectation), but be grateful that they think of your needs and let them know that you notice. Appreciate someone's thoughtfulness. When your spouse comes home in the evening, thank them for working so hard; if your children have something to share, listen to them. If they have worked hard on something difficult for them, thank them for making the effort. And most importantly, don't let your appreciation be limited to what they do for you, but appreciate who they are. None of us want to be ignored for who we are or be expected to give what we don't have or don't know about.

11 Trust

Definition attributed to Oxford Dictionary
   Trust: A firm belief or confidence in the honesty, integrity, reliability, and justice of another person or thing; faith; reliance

There can be no trust without an expectation of truth. Truth is the foundation of trust. We would never consciously extend our trust to someone that deceives us. But without being sure if there is truth in your interaction, having trust becomes an act of faith. Trust brings us up close and personal to one another as you have removed the barriers you believe protect you. You are willing to risk that intimacy because you want to have faith in the person you are sharing with. Faith that they will respect your vulnerability or at least have faith in what guided you to extend that trust. Because it's difficult to open up to one another, our circles of trust are very small. The secrets we hold so tightly may have less to do with the subjects of the secrets than with ensuring we will be respected. People are ridiculed and considered naive or childish when they indiscriminately trust. We are taught to be on guard, to protect ourselves by automatically assuming we will be hurt or taken advantage of.
   We hoard our trust because we know so little about one another. We may choose instead to be guarded, distrustful and keep others at arm's length; in that way, we feel in charge of our emotional security. But if we desire healthy connections and relationships, we need to be willing to extend some trust. Take some risks. Announce (at least to

yourself) your intent to be truthful so the communication begins on an honest footing.

Trusting is a difficult thing to do, especially if you have been badly hurt. But you can begin by realizing that those hurtful experiences were not a judgment of you but the expression of someone else's fear. And you made the choice that put you there. Having said that, anytime you repeat an experience that resulted in the same pain or disappointment over and over again, you may need to take a look at the choices you are making. Our subconscious choices will always bring us to the same result until we finally make a conscious decision about what is healthy for us. For example, we may be attracted to certain personalities. That attraction deceives us that "this time it will be different." But each time, you get hurt. Your attractions and choices don't change, and the results don't change either. Nothing about it will change until you finally recognize that what has become normal for you isn't necessarily safe or healthy. What changes it is recognizing your part in it and making different choices. But again, that means changing how you feel about yourself, choosing from a more powerful place, a place where you know you are deserving of something better.

Repeating past trauma only indicates that healing still evades you. Your trust and your time are valuable gifts. But as a gift, trust should be freely given. If it is only a loan, extend only what you are emotionally capable of giving or losing. Don't coat your trust in expectations. You can believe in the inherent goodness of people, but whether they are able to be as good as you see them isn't up to you. If someone extends their trust (their truth) to you, honor it, and don't disvalue their truth by gossiping, judging, or demeaning them because of what they shared.

It has been said that everyone has an emotional bank account and that trust is the "interest" gained over time. Deception and disappointment drain that account, "spending" the trust gained, ultimately bankrupting the account. This holds true with any relationship, whether it is personal, business, or social. When you disrespect someone, you withdraw from that account, and they will emotionally, economically, or physically pull away. Expectations are also withdrawals, eroding away love and respect. This is especially true within your family, where interactions are constant, and the opportunities are endless. Truth and trust in one another to be truthful can be the most important component in any relationship and is what builds emotional security. Repeated disrespect makes it progressively harder to regain that trust. Like the boy that cries wolf, eventually, others stop listening. The account will be bankrupt.

When someone proves to be untrustworthy, lies, and treats others with disrespect, they only attract disrespect in return. They will always assume the worst in others because they see that tendency within themselves. A liar always assumes that others are lying. A thief fears losing what they have because they take from others. Many people who habitually lie believe trust and truth are irrelevant, only a means to an end, and a belief that the end justifies the means. And that is all they will be left with is "the end," not the journey.

"We're never so vulnerable than when we trust someone – but paradoxically, if we cannot trust, neither can we find love or joy."

—*Walter Anderson*

"We must cease striving and trust God to provide what He thinks is best and in whatever time He chooses to make it available. But this kind of trusting doesn't come naturally. It's a spiritual crisis of the will in which we must choose to exercise faith."

—*Charles R. Swindoll*

To cease striving we must be patient and have trust in the moments that find us. Because in many ways we have called for them and the truth they contain. The chosen time is now.

12 Intent

Communication is all about expressing need. Not just material or emotional needs but also the need for understanding. Our needs are reflected in everything we do. Every gesture or expectation, verbal or non-verbal, intentional or not, is an effort to get our needs met or to be truly understood. That same dance of need and intent is true for all levels of human interaction. What is true for individuals is also true for the collective "us" as corporations, communities, and government. It's important to realize that all communication, whether personal, political, commercial, or informative has an author, and every author has intent or is working to express the intent of others. Thinking consciously, you should always consider that intent and read between the lines of what is communicated. You may not be able to determine whether the message is true, but the intent can be discerned. Doing that, you can make decisions based on the intent of the message rather than solely on its content which may be designed to deceive.

"Learn what is true in order to do what is right."

—*Thomas Henry Huxley*

Advertisers tell us what they think we want to hear to meet their need to make a profit. A less-than-scrupulous man may tell a woman that he loves her to get sexually involved. All of us, at some time or another, have been dishonest about our intentions. We feel we will fail to get what we want by simply asking for it, so we look for other ways to take it, even when it is at another's expense. Communication, by its nature, is manipulative; it is trying to connect or coerce us in some way. Perhaps to convince or convey an understanding. It can be truthful or misleading, but there is always intent. In sharing something true about ourselves, our intent is to be understood. But behind that is our need, which can be as simple as the need to make a connection. The need to be accepted, to justify our thinking, or to ask for help or trust. There is always intent; intent is the active part of the need reaching out to be satisfied. Just as words are powerful and should be used respectfully, our intent should also be respectful. Intent can help you identify what you need but crafting your words to influence another is manipulation. Manipulation may get you what you want but never what you need.

13 What is True?

Facts may be defined as things that are known or proved to be true through calculation and experience. Truth as a concept may include fact but can also include belief. But belief, by its nature, doesn't require proof or fact. We are free to believe anything to be true without a scientific study proving its existence.

But truth and fact are sometimes used interchangeably, but when it is said that "truth is in the eye of the beholder," it is true that each of us *perceives* truth differently depending upon our experiences. So, personal truth is really judgment. Our perception of what is true is the culmination of our personal or collective experiences, which obviously differ from one person to the next. We subconsciously accept many things as true without bothering to question their factual nature. But in discerning the truth of something, we evaluate it against what we have already accepted or have a belief about. And we are generally reluctant to accept anything that casts doubt upon what we already believe.

But the easiest way to know the truth of yourself is to begin with your emotions. *How you feel is real; how you came to feel that way is true.* By checking in about the true origin of your feelings, you can respond appropriately and not just react to the situation. The memories created at that moment help you respond better next time. That only takes an extra moment. Truth isn't far away. Although searching for it may seem like a long journey, you know right away when you are happy or sad and afraid. Don't be so quick to deny your feelings. Trust your "gut instinct." There is strength in your own nature to understand what is true, and you should rely on it rather than on the counsel of others.

> *"Never apologize for showing feeling. When you do so, you apologize for the truth."*
>
> —Benjamin Disraeli

Although truth seems vital to our ability to make informed decisions, it is also vital to a functioning society. It is vital to be able to discern the truth of political rhetoric, propaganda, and marketing, all of which seek to manipulate you. A politician may make a statement undeniably true for him *personally* that, when used to project the same truth in a broader sense, is patently false. For example, if a politician states that money spent benefits "Americans," it may be true enough for him because he is American, and it did benefit him, even though it may not help the majority of people. As spoken, that "truth" is a manipulation that is intentionally misleading in the context it was describing. There are professionals paid a lot of money to "spin the truth" because to announce something as true or to insinuate truth gives the message value and legality. Unfortunately, we seem more than ready to believe whatever we are told and less inclined to question the messenger. It is easier to accept what we already believe than to see things differently or question our vision.

> *"Without seeking, truth cannot be known at all. It can neither be declared from pulpits, nor set down in articles, nor in any wise prepared and sold in packages ready for use."*
>
> —John Ruskin

> *"Nothing is so firmly believed as what we least know."*
>
> —Montaigne

People place so much importance on their version of the truth that when it's questioned, it becomes a trigger for them, as if it is challenging the entirety of who they are. Even with all of our searching for the truth of humanity, we still seem at a loss to get to know the truth of ourselves. Perhaps it is one and the same, and why the big questions of our humanity go unanswered.

If you experience doubt, don't condemn yourself and feel you are betraying your belief; think of it simply as an invitation to think a little deeper. Use your anxiety as a steppingstone; see where it leads. Any ideas that are considered can enrich your understanding. Critical thinking involves being open, suspending judgment, and examining intent, your own or others. Don't cherry-pick only the ideas that justify what you know now. Be willing to entertain thoughts that are different, especially if you are being pressured not to. Ideas are not the enemy. Those who seek to restrict the expression of the truth only do so to justify their own beliefs or further an agenda.

The stronger your reaction is to something, the more you can learn about yourself. Once you begin to reflect on what it is you really feel, you can acknowledge why you are reacting that way. For example, if you feel defensive, then you are afraid. Fear is easily identifiable this way, and that feeling is true.

There are natural physical laws we have accepted as true or science has proven. Laws of motion, matter, cause and effect, and physics. But at this moment, how you feel, where you stand, and who you are is true and indisputable. Each moment, you bring all your memories to bear on a situation to form an opinion of what you are experiencing. But the truth is in the moment, naked and immediate, untroubled by your past, uninformed by opinion. It is pure and immutable and is only revealed by being authentically present at the moment without those judgments. Your emotions can come close to disclosing the truth, but your emotions are influenced by your memories and prejudices. So, don't necessarily believe your thinking is clear and uncluttered because it is very difficult to undo all that comes attached to your thoughts. So, until you can discern the moment clearly, to some degree at least, recognize the part your bias and prejudices play in your understanding, you can only know that your "truth" is a personal one, a judgment, and as such isn't necessarily true.

"Truth is not what you want it to be; it is what it is, and you must bend to its power or live a lie."

—Miyamoto Musashi

---

14 Belief and Awareness

Belief can be defined as acceptance of something as true. That doesn't mean it is true, but we have accepted it and extended our faith and trust in it. Our beliefs become hardwired to our self-concept and ego. We define ourselves by what we believe. At times, even scientific proof cannot dissuade us. In your need to believe, you will avoid anything that challenges it. So, if another's beliefs challenge your own, you may consider their beliefs wrong or bad, judging others harshly who don't believe as you do. We become so protective of our beliefs we go to war to defend them. But if multitudes of people worldwide believe in multiple ways, we should recognize that belief is merely a choice we make. Whatever truth is there is personal. So, we should not equate belief with absolute truth, nor should our search for truth end with our beliefs.

"Believe nothing, O monks, merely because you have been told it… or because it is traditional, or because you yourselves have imagined it. Do not believe what your teacher tells you merely out of respect for the teacher. But whatsoever, after due examination and analysis, you find to be conducive to the good, the benefit, the welfare of all beings—that doctrine believe and cling to and take it as your guide."

—*Buddha*

On the other hand, awareness is the state of being conscious of something, directly perceiving or being cognizant of a fundamental experience. Awareness happens in seconds before we pass judgment on what we see and react to it. When we first become aware of something and are able to postpone our reaction, we may give the truth a chance to appear. Stretch out the moment, be clear about what you are feeling, and don't rush to react. The moment of awareness is where truth resides. At that moment, if we haven't reacted or passed judgment on it, the truth may be found. To go one step further, if we develop our awareness to accept whatever comes before us, we may allow the experience to be what it is. We can observe without judgment.

"Nobody can impose your beliefs on you. It's always you who in the last instance, can permit a belief to be true for you or not."

—*Marc Reklau*

"The first step toward change is awareness. The second step is acceptance."

—*Nathaniel Branden*

"The key to growth is the introduction of higher dimensions of consciousness into our awareness."

—*Lao Tzu*

---

15 Good Versus Bad

As we experience life from moment to moment, our memories assign good and bad qualities to what we experience. And these qualities become labels, 'this was good' or 'this was bad.' And by attaching those labels to your memories, you apply those qualities to each new moment that is in some way similar to that memory. We may collectively agree on what good and bad experiences are, but that agreement only fixes us in place and doesn't allow for other possibilities. The concepts of good and bad are only judgments, but they are also how we categorize our experiences and decide where to place our attention. What we decide is good attracts us and reaffirms us. We tend to avoid, disbelieve, or disvalue what we question or judge as bad. But those judgments are entirely subjective, not real, not true. Those that live in the Arctic may experience 20-degree weather as a warm day, although you may consider it frigid. The truth is that it is twenty degrees; whether that is cold or warm is a point of view.

"Bad" situations sometimes bring "good" things, and what we perceive as good may lead us to sorrow. Our habitual judgment perpetuates stress and expectation and prejudices us from experiencing things ultimately valuable to our understanding. What may inconvenience or repulse you may be another's joy. We *can* accept what the world brings us without judgment. Acceptance is growth. Maintaining that our view is the only truth that matters only illustrates our lack of compassion and limits our relationships with those who think as we do. Perhaps we should consider that there is no good and bad at all, but only God. If God is all and created all, then bad was never created and only exists in how we define it and our belief in it. And that applies to what we see as 'good' as well.

It is vitally important to consider these concepts. Because our inability to go beyond them will interfere with the moment as it presents itself. We can't know the future, but we can choose how we will face it before it even arrives. If you judge that a certain situation will be negative or challenge you, you will shut down. You can't search for what is true when you already have decided ahead of time what you will consider. Just accept life as life, a moment for the moment, without judgment.

Start recognizing your propensity to classify your experiences and stop yourself when you begin to judge. Start reminding yourself that life has brought you what you need in each moment to grow and understand. Sometimes moments are hard to accept, but that doesn't make them wrong or bad. Especially when the moments are difficult, they offer us something. Your car may have a flat tire that makes you late for work; it may inconvenience you or frighten you in some way, but perhaps that situation changes your day in a way that will benefit you. Perhaps being delayed has kept you away from an accident on your route. Try to be thankful for those random situations; they may not be as random as you think. When you refrain from judging every moment, the benefit of what you experience becomes clear. There is a reason for the things we experience; a reason that reveals itself over time.

"People like to say that the conflict is between good and evil. The real conflict is between truth and lies."

—*Don Miguel Ruiz*

"Nature has no principles. She makes no distinction between good and evil."

—*Anatole France*

"When the divine vision is attained, all appear equal; and there remains no distinction of good or bad, or of high and low."

—*Ramakrishna*

16 Truth and Prejudice

The best way to become self-aware is through our interactions with one another. We naturally tend to size each other up based on our culture and experience. If it is obvious that we have things in common, we feel an immediate level of comfort and trust in how our words and actions will be interpreted. Conversely, when we view someone as different, we become uneasy because we can't predict how we will be received. When something is unknown, it becomes threatening to some degree. When we see others, we begin by immediately categorizing who we *believe* the other person to be. And those judgments may block our willingness to interact on an equal level. The opportunity to communicate in a good way may be stifled or eliminated entirely.

"Most often people see in life occasions for persisting in their opinions rather than for educating themselves."
—André Gide

"Few people are capable of expressing with equanimity opinions that differ from the prejudices of their social environment. Most people are incapable of forming such opinions."
—Albert Einstein

When you judge someone, you are not trying to understand the truth of a person but only justifying your rejection or acceptance of them. The act of judging closes the door to understanding. When you judge someone, you are looking for reasons to exclude them. And even if you accept them, you may only be accepting what you believe about them and neglecting opportunities to understand one another on a less superficial level.

> *"The greatest friend of Truth is Time, her greatest enemy is Prejudice, and her constant companion Humility."*
> —*Charles Caleb Colton*

If you are not a victim of it, it's easy to feel that prejudice isn't that big a deal. We all have the right to limit our association to whom we choose and believe what we want. But that 'right' (which in practice creates a lot of 'wrong') ignores just how much damage prejudice causes within a community and to one other personally. Prejudice is never justified. We establish laws against it. It is set in our national Constitution that we are all equal. And when you do feel prejudice directed toward you, there is no denying the truth of how that feels. It has become part of human history and wars, our attitudes always attacking our differences and the inhumanity of man.

> *"Prejudice is a burden that confuses the past, threatens the future, and renders the present inaccessible"*
> —*Maya Angelou*

> *"Prejudice… means you don't see the other human being anymore, but only your concept of that human being. To reduce the aliveness of another human being to a concept is already a form of violence."*
> —*Eckhart Tolle*

So, any differences we perceive create ideal scapegoats for our fear. Differences in the way we have been born into this world or the beliefs we have accepted. Prejudice makes us all victims. Only when we suspend judgment of others can progress be made personally and as a society.

No one ever knows another without sharing, and when we push others away, no sharing is possible. Sharing shouldn't be limited to only those things that categorize us and feed our prejudices but sharing what is real about us. Try going beyond the pattern of thinking that limits you. Choose to share something more personal than your job, religion, or where you are from. Don't automatically feel the need to validate your beliefs. Share some deeper aspects of yourself, perhaps how you are feeling at that moment or a personal experience. Ask questions and share to better understand, not to label. Maybe instead of affirming our place, we could be finding our place with each other.

It is difficult to totally refrain from judgment, but we can be true about it. You can silently acknowledge that you are judging someone and realize that what you think you know doesn't make it true. Instead, extend some compassion and be humble. Don't look for how you might be better than another. But recognize that, at that moment, we are all just people. We are all people of color; white is a color as well. We remain just people when we stop judging. People who may even be someone important to you if you let them. Remember that even if you are quiet about your prejudices, you still project them. You are still building a wall, not opening a door, and the other person can and does feel it.

"Prejudice cannot see things that are because it is always looking for things that aren't."

—Unknown

Prejudice creates ready-made scapegoats for our insecurity, easily creating a threat where none exists. That's why prejudice and fear are such powerful tools of propaganda. It takes your irrational fears and gives them a face. We may take pride in being identified or labeled in a specific way. Our labels become emotional anchors to our societal, cultural, racial, political, or religious identities. We can say, "I am a Democrat, Republican, Hispanic, Catholic, Christian, Muslim, Jewish, Native, Black, Caucasian, straight, gay, northerner, southerner, New Yorker, Californian, rich, poor, laborer, stockbroker," any number of ways we want to identify ourselves and categorize others. We apply those labels to believe we know something of another. He's one of us, or he's not one of us. Prejudice is not just judging other races or cultures but feeling justified in our hatred and distrust of anyone with whom we don't feel kinship. Prejudice is not a happy feeling; it is not kind or loving. It is fear and ignorance and doesn't serve you in any way or protect you. When your beliefs are based upon anger, hatred, judgment, and violence, no good comes of it.

    The biggest danger is when we believe that our prejudices give us license to enact violence and injustice against those targeted by our fear. Having to live constantly in defense of one's wrong thinking can make for a bitter and angry existence. And there are a lot of bitter and angry people out there. A bigot is devoted to their opinion to the extent that they take pride in their ignorance and are actually eager to be hateful rather than compassionate and to feel superior rather than humble. When you take pride in your ignorance, you have labeled yourself that. You become someone easily manipulated because you are constantly looking for justification for those beliefs, and anyone that feeds you what you already believe will be able to sway you for their purposes.

"What does a bigot do when he meets someone who challenges his opinions? He doesn't give. He stays rigid. Doesn't even try to listen, just lashes out."

—Harper Lee

And it isn't just individuals aligning with hate. All of us need to be aware of what ideals we lend ourselves to. The groups, communities, and belief systems we choose to align ourselves with should not demand our steadfast allegiance or set us against one another. If we are committed to becoming better people, we cannot condone the actions of those who contribute to the suffering of others.

"Anger and intolerance are the enemies of correct understanding."

—*Mahatma Gandhi*

"Fear is the only true enemy, born of ignorance and the parent of anger and hate."

—*Edward Albert*

Those with power and authority wield prejudice and stereotypes as weapons of influence and persuasion. For example, you may never meet someone from a Middle Eastern country but freely identify people from that part of the world as violent extremists. You are not just prejudging someone you don't even know but have been coerced into fearing an entire nation of people. Promoting those stereotypes only serves those that want to instill fear or go to war, and their intent is always greed. There is no need to promote hate unless it winds up benefiting the promoter in some way.

There are always differences between us to one degree or another. If you begin to see that some behaviors and interactions are just cultural, that may take away some of the threat you feel. You are you, and that's all you need to be. That's all any of us need to be. It isn't necessary to get to know everyone you meet, but when you meet someone and start to label them, let that go and just silently wish them well. Recognizing prejudice in ourselves and others is important to the truth because it isn't just another set of lies but an attack on one another. We live in a world with an incredible diversity of cultures we can learn from, so whether you travel abroad or not, you can "cultivate" a worldly perspective by seeing that what we have in common is our humanity. Extend the moments that we allow one another our humanity.

"Diversity… is not casual liberal tolerance of anything not yourself. It is not polite accommodation. Instead, diversity is, in action, the sometimes-painful awareness that other people, other races, other voices, other habits of mind have as much integrity of being, as much claim on the world as you do… And I urge you, amid all the differences present to the eye and mind, to reach out to create the bond that… will protect us all. We are all meant to be here together."

—*William Chase*

"To know the true reality of yourself, you must be aware not only of your conscious thoughts, but also of your unconscious prejudices, bias and habits."

—*Unknown*

17 Community

Community can be expressed and defined in many ways; sometimes, community is related to our cultural identity. Or a small community of family and close friends. Spiritual communities are made up of people that are like-minded on matters of humanity and spirit and, to some extent, agree on a common dogma or creed, whereas business communities are based upon common markets (be they local or global) and common needs, but not necessarily common philosophies.

At its best, spontaneous communities can occur during catastrophes where our truest needs connect us. We have all witnessed news footage of natural disasters where people are working together, helping one another despite their differences. It no longer matters what their skin color or culture is. Need becomes the commonality between strangers, breaking down social barriers. In moments of tragedy, we willingly accept the support of strangers. We set our differences and prejudices aside to tend to one another. If we can do that then why can't we do it now? But when calamity strikes and needs are so obvious, there is no intent or expectation; we can be certain that we *will be led to where we are called.*

That sense of responsibility to one another can be painfully intimate, and it can humble us, especially when we finally see our prejudices for what they are. The walls between us fall when we can relate to one another's suffering. There are no expectations involved because we cannot envision where help will come from. But happily, it is not only tragedy that can break down our barriers. There can also be times of joy and celebration, like the birth of a child or a marriage or the end of war or conflict, which can unite us communally. True community extends the concept of family in its best form, including us all to a common end. Is it possible to voluntarily set aside our prejudices to make those communities we seek? There is evidence of that in worship settings, workplaces, non-profits, and other examples, all usually under the guise of truth and service. But without a foundation of truth, there can be no trust. Without trust, we won't allow ourselves to be vulnerable. Without some vulnerability, it is difficult, if not impossible, to share who we are.

"If you think only of yourself, if you forget the rights and well-being of others, or, worse still, if you exploit others, ultimately you will lose. You will have no friends who will show concern for your well-being. Moreover, if a tragedy befalls you, instead of feeling concerned, others might even secretly rejoice. By contrast, if an individual is compassionate and altruistic, and has the interests of others in mind, then irrespective of whether that person knows a lot of people, wherever that person moves, he or she will immediately make friends. And when that person faces a tragedy, there will be plenty of people who will come to help."

—The XIV Dalai Lama

"A true community is not just about being geographically close to someone or part of the same social web network. It's about feeling connected and responsible for what happens. Humanity is our ultimate community, and everyone plays a crucial role."

—Yehuda Berg

---

18 Challenging Ourselves

Why should we challenge ourselves? Each moment is an opportunity to choose your next step, your next word, even your intent. You challenge yourself daily in the kinds of choices you make. We commonly set ourselves on a course of action. Challenge ourselves to increase our physical fitness, diet, reduce our dependence on tobacco or alcohol, fix our relationships, or express our talent. We challenge ourselves to create a better version of ourselves. None of those things are easy, yet we dive in with the expectation that if we achieve them, we will be happy, healthier, more attractive, and stronger. But to challenge what we believe to be true about us? As they say, "There's the rub." We may know we should change certain behaviors, but to do the mental and emotional work to actually be the person we envision is beyond the appetite of most. As long as we can make ourselves appear as we want to be seen, most don't consider putting in the work to actually become that.

How we decide to act and whether that action serves others or only ourselves indicates what we value. Our actions, not words, project and form our true character. You may not intend ahead of time to help someone, but you rise to their need anyway because that is the right thing to do. Putting others ahead of ourselves reduces the egotistic hold on our thinking. If, on top of that, we can cultivate conscious thinking and better our understanding of ourselves, we will be contributing to a better world and blessing all around us.

The challenge should be to cultivate your character and integrity. Not just to be healthy physically but mentally and spiritually as well. In being truthful, worthy of trust, respectful, kind, and generous without reservation or expectation are all things you can do and be without cost. Even unvoiced, your intentions still go out into the world. You never escape responsibility for your thinking. Your thoughts and intentions go ahead of you and define you.

"Watch your thoughts, they become words.
Watch your words, they become actions
Watch your actions, they become habits
Watch your habits, they become character
Watch your character, it becomes your destiny."

—Unknown

Our intent should be to tread lightly with each other, not intend harm or confusion or seek control. You are probably already a kind person, so that shouldn't be a challenge. But our personal relationship with truth is like any other relationship with all the expected ups and downs. And it is inevitable that sooner or later, you'll find aspects of yourself where truth hits closest to the bone, and you may not be ready to resurrect those memories or deal with those triggers. Truth is easy when telling it doesn't matter. But it is the sharpest stones in our path that hide the gold. When you are threatened, you may have enough self-control to refrain from lying, but you may still reach out for any excuse to avoid the encounter entirely. But even in recognizing your avoidance, you are well on your way to controlling your mind and your response. The challenge will always be found in your willingness to examine what makes you tick. Even just thinking about your reluctance to make changes, you are applying yourself to the challenge.

When you understand that your subconscious drives a lot of your reactions, you'll realize that there still will be parts of your life on autopilot. When something attracts your awareness, you may feel called to think consciously about it. But most of your daily experiences may not call to you that way. You may have no desire to understand what drives you to act and gladly blame others for every misfortune you experience. I believe it is a fact of humanity that we must feel backed into a corner full of pain and confusion before the desire is awakened to fully understand what caused us to be there. Those desperate times are the proverbial "cracks in the armor" that may drive your desire for change. But unfortunately, that desire may only last until the current crisis is abated. We all have many "come to Jesus" moments in our lives that tend to fade once the need passes. But perhaps enough cumulative stresses have come your way that your search for immediate relief grows into a full-blown desire for a different way of life.

"Nothing ever goes away until it has taught us what we need to know."

—*Pema Chodron*

"There came a time when the risk to remain tight in the bud was more painful than the risk it took to blossom."

—*Anaïs Nin*

As this quote so beautifully captures, avoiding the truth may bring you to a place you may feel is too painful to bear. Like a woman giving birth, ultimately, we have no choice; *it is the nature of every living thing to grow and bloom.* Finally, making the conscious decision to find a better way feels like a wonderful release, no matter how arduous the internal journey may seem.

"Most of the critical things in life, which become the starting points for human destiny, are little things."

—*R. Smith*

So, understand that in accepting this challenge, you will be up against your most powerful adversary, your own mind. You have spent years protecting and defending your thoughts, beliefs, and actions. But bit by bit, each time you reflect on the truth of your feelings, it will be easier. You will come to know how being real and telling the truth is true freedom. You will attract beneficial consequences to your life. You will notice that when you become more comfortable with the truth, people will react differently to you. Some will be attracted to you. Others may back away because how they see themselves reflected in you, how different you are from them, makes them uncomfortable. So even if you speak with kindness and compassionate intent, the truth may be seen as confrontational to those who are challenged by it. Remember, they, too, are trying to hide. But do not take it as a call to war; you don't need to convince anyone of what you have found. The truth will do its work with or without your defense of it. The challenge you have accepted is not a competition and does not pit you against anyone or anyone else's beliefs. Our spiritual purpose in this world does have a physical and emotional cost. When we let go of what was, we have to ensure that what we replace it with is in line with our values and commit ourselves to it. Some things we believed were important to us may be difficult to let go of. But sometimes, it is in letting go that we gain so much.

19 Our Physical Nature

In my experience, the relationship we have with our surroundings is a basic tenet to understanding ourselves. What is true within us is also true of our environment. The functions of life around us are also within us. The natural world is the one place that meets us honestly and gives us the clearest reflection of ourselves. When we take a walk in the forest, our minds are unpolluted by the mechanizations and intent of others. We can tune in to ourselves by tuning out the modern world and all the things that grab our attention. There is a quietness in the natural world that calls to our own silence. There is an awareness that moves us without our judgments. An awareness that is a natural part of us and a yearning that is manifested as growth.

Ancient cultures were attuned to the environment for survival. Over time humans began to create the conditions they needed to survive rather than just reacting to the conditions they found themselves in. What couldn't be explained or controlled, they attributed to a spiritual realm. A spiritual dimension that still calls to us. All of life has that spiritual dimension to it. But what we find in the diversity of nature is lost in our man-made environments. Modern environments aren't alive. They can only tell us what we already know. They can only tell us the answers we have programmed into them. So divorced from nature, man is now more attuned to a wilderness of emotion and economic need. Survival now revolves more around our emotional and intellectual strength than our physical strength. The human struggle remains, but it is a mental struggle, not a physical one.

> *"The energy of the mind is the essence of life."*
> —*Aristotle*

The flight or fight survival mechanism that served us so well in the natural world has been turned inward against ourselves. We still use the responses of prehistoric man to deal with our modern fears and create make-believe monsters to defend ourselves against.

> *"Challenging the meaning of life is the truest expression of the state of being human."*
> —*Viktor E. Frankl*

We are quickly coming to a point where we have changed the environment to the extent that it cannot sustain us any longer, and the consequences will continue to grow. The environment mirrors our mental dysmorphia. Everything is out of balance. In our yearning for truth, we want the answers provided to us as if man has created the answers and only man can provide them. But that does not mean we will ever find them there. If we have a question about our place and purpose in the world, if we have the eyes to see and ears to hear, we can find our answers in the simplest forms of nature. How many spiritual truths have been found focusing on a lotus flower? Nothing humbles us so much as coming face to face with the enormity of nature. We realize how small and insignificant we are. We believe we are all-powerful until we are caught in a storm. And it shows us that all parts of us are truly insignificant except our ability to love and remember where we came from. Maybe that's what spirituality is, the process of experiencing our own nature.

"And this, our life, exempt from public haunt, find tongues in trees, books in running brooks, sermons in stones, and good in everything."

—William Shakespeare

"Irrespective of your belief system, there are certain forces that act upon us and make us do what we do, ironically human race is the only breed who is more susceptible to it and we keep denying it."

—Ramana Permmaraju

20 Signs and Symbols

Anything we see can transform into the answer we seek if we look at it with that intention and allow it to be symbolic of what is within us. Symbols are shortcuts to our psyche. The ability to recognize something as symbolic of something else is part of the maturation of thought, where we gain the ability to understand abstract concepts. Even learning to read is a process of deciphering abstract symbols.

Symbols are designed to interact with our awareness to visually communicate an idea. And only work when we agree on their meaning. They may be designed to guide our behavior, like in advertising or directional signs, but commonly represent beliefs or allegiances. Think of common symbols like a traffic sign, a swastika, an advertising logo, a ring, a flag, a cross, school colors, a written word, all the many things whose meanings we all agree upon.

In ancient times, we had no real grasp of the scientific reality of the natural world. It either provided for us or threatened us. That in itself could be agreed upon and were easily symbolic concepts. Concepts that could be assigned to objects and creatures carry symbolic meanings and spiritual qualities. When the nature of something didn't have an explanation, we could assign it whatever value we saw in it. Good harvests and fruits became symbolic of the Creator blessing our efforts, spring a symbol of new life. Everything in this world reflected different aspects of our nature back to us. There was recognition that we are a part, not apart, from the natural world.

"All nature is a vast symbolism: Every material fact has sheathed within it a spiritual truth."

—*Edwin Powell Hubble*

Symbols convey concepts without language. Some are created to lead the observer on a spiritual path. The mandalas of the Far East are symbols that, when used in meditation, guide us in prayer by illustrating the qualities needed to attain enlightenment. The Om symbol refers to the breath of the universe. The stylized eye in the Middle East is symbolic of spiritual insight and higher knowledge. The cross symbolizes self-sacrifice and eternal life, a symbol that was used prior to Christianity itself. The art and regalia of native peoples represent the spiritual nature of those animals and birds that are being honored and embody the wearer with those spiritual qualities. Art is symbolic expression. Anytime we reflect on the meaning of what we are presented with visually or even musically, it can take us deeper into ourselves. Even our memories become a type of symbol as they represent how we should feel when we meet an experience again.

"All nature is a vast symbolism: Every material fact has sheathed within it a spiritual truth."

—*Edwin Powell Hubble*

"Every natural fact is a symbol of some spiritual fact."

—*Ralph Waldo Emerson*

Some symbols have been created or co-opted to be a rallying cry for prejudice and fear. Think of the patriotism surrounding a national flag. Or a crowd of people carrying signs with peace symbols or bearing the countenance of a popular leader. You don't have to "translate" a symbol's meaning for it to have an influence on your thoughts. Some people hold fast to certain symbols to represent their allegiance to specific groups or causes or superstitiously ward off evil or bring them luck. But if symbols have power, it is only in one's belief of what they represent, not the symbol itself. One example is the swastika, a symbol hundreds of years old and used by Hindus, Buddhists, and Asian and American tribes as a symbol of good luck and well-being, but much later, it was appropriated by Hitler's Third Reich as an Aryan symbol of fascism. And that use was so insidious that it lost its original meaning.

So, you can recognize that the function of symbolism can be either to explain the unexplainable or as a placeholder for an idea. But also realize the extent to which these things have been woven into our lives, and that they are all created by someone, and that someone had an intent in mind.

"Symbolism is the language of the Mysteries. By symbols men have ever sought to communicate to each other those thoughts which transcend the limitations of language."

—*Manly Hall*

---

21   To Act in Loving Ways

Perhaps you see now that all your actions have an origin, an intention, or a memory that sets things into motion. You may not consciously intend anything specific and are just reacting to the situation, but your need will drive you to act in ways to meet it. A common refrain is, "That's just who I am." Now maybe you can see that it's how you have chosen to be. You have chosen it because you have allowed your intentions to run unchecked and your memories to determine the present.

There are only two real emotions in life, love, and fear. Everything stems from one or the other. You may do things to or for one another out of fear (obligation, expectation, need) or out of love (caring, commitment, empathy, respect). You can be responsible with your actions by asking yourself whether what you are doing or how you are behaving is loving or defensive. Once you acknowledge your true motivation, you can easily see why people react to you the way they do. When you understand that, it becomes easier to forgive others because you know it is fear that is causing their aggression and anger. Fear of being challenged, fear of being seen, of being hurt, as well as being inadequate. In understanding that, you can be compassionate instead of reactive. Find the love that is there or needed and nurture it.

So, not only are love and fear the driving force of our actions, but they are the filters through which we see the world. When you look from a place of fear, you create threats to justify your feelings. When we look at the world in a compassionate way, we see others' needs and act in ways that support one another. Our smallest actions, especially the non-verbal ones, are emotional vibrations you broadcast. Are you sending out love and caring or fear and pain? You can quickly feel someone's "vibes" without trying too hard to do so. Your spouse doesn't have to say, "I do this because I love you," for you to know it's true. You know when someone is 'in a bad mood' without even interacting with them. You can start recognizing moments in that way, seeing someone's actions as an expression of their love or expression of their fear. If we can step back and look at each other in that way, we may be more responsible with our attitudes and more understanding of others. As an example of what we carry with us: picture an empty room.

One person enters full of anger, and that anger permeates the atmosphere in the room, others can feel it and will begin reacting toward it or avoid it entirely. Versus another person entering the room with joy and happiness, and that joy will fill that space and lift everyone in it. The space doesn't change, but the energy does. Energy that attracts or repels us. That is what we fill our homes with, our energy. That is what people will experience there. When they say, "It feels so good to be here," it's true. They will feel welcome, protected, and safe, but it is not the structure of the space that makes them feel that way but the 'structure of emotions' that reside there.

True love is not conditional or unintentional. We must intend to love and intend to act in a loving way by putting others' needs before our own. Having empathy means you not only sense others' emotions but are willing to imagine what they may be going through. Communicating can be a loving gesture when we listen to one another. Love is a verb, an action. To love. Love is something we do and must feed every day to have it in our lives. You know which gestures and words are loving and which are manipulative. You should meet one another's needs because it is a loving thing to do, not because you are expected to do it. It is not tit for tat. In giving freely, you will receive; in loving, you will be loved. Love evolves and changes because the truth of us evolves and changes.

> *"Isn't it a pity? Isn't it a shame?*
> *How we break each other's hearts*
> *Cause each other pain?*
> *How we take each other's love*
> *Without thinking anymore?*
> *Forgetting to give back*
> *Isn't it a pity?"*
>
> —George Harrison

> *"Love is a sacred reserve of energy; it is like the blood of spiritual evolution."*
>
> —Teilhard de Chardin

Loving is a choice. You can say "I love you" as much as you want, but if you act disrespectfully, it is clearly not true. Realize just how much you communicate non-verbally. Think of when you give the "cold shoulder" to someone when displeased or cuddle up close when you want some intimacy. Silence says as much as your words. Don't let competing needs and arguments exist silently at the core of your family interactions. Everyone can agree on how much misunderstanding hurts. Walking around with unresolved feelings and issues makes you feel like you are treading on broken glass being around one another. You don't know what to do; you just know you want to feel better. But healing requires effort and vulnerability. Being open to seeing the other's point of view is a loving gesture. Being loving and open to someone's truth means we are willing to risk casting doubt on our own understanding. If your objective is only to gain agreement, to win an argument, the satisfaction will be fleeting, the circumstances unresolved. Trying to win an argument only focuses your attention on what you fear. Winning connotates a battle. In arguments, we want to be "right," but more often, we just want to feel heard and understood.

We can act in loving ways in all our interactions. Even in disagreement or pain, we can still find compassion and support one another with kind words, kind actions, and kind, selfless decisions. Kindness should not just be reserved for our families or only depend upon what we get in return. Waiting or expecting to be rewarded for our good deeds isn't loving; it is expectation.

"Love without action is meaningless and action without love is irrelevant."

—*Deepak Chopra*

When you are compassionate, you aren't afraid or expecting to be repaid. When you aren't afraid, you can be real. When you are real, you are acting consciously. Love is the breathing in of life. Fear leaves us breathless.

"I've learned that people will forget what you've said, people will forget what you did, but they will never forget the way you made them feel."

—*Maya Angelou*

"Sharing how you feel what's real for you may be scary... But every time you hold back truth, you make fear more important than love. This is why the depth of your ability to love will always be mirrored by your ability to be honest. It's really as simple as that."

—*Mark Groves*

22 The Need for Connection

As isolated as we have become in this day and age, sometimes never even knowing our own neighbors, the basic human need for relationships is being neglected. Cyber or internet "relationships" are fulfilling some of that need for those truly isolated by geography or physical impairment. Two-dimensional experiences may have changed the nature of connection, but don't shield us from consequences and are a poor substitute for meaningful interaction. Any time we make a choice sends us in a different direction, and that direction in itself is a consequence of our choice, but when we are not face to face with those we interact with, we can pretend we are protected from our behavior. We can say what we want, and no one can find us. The physical threat doesn't exist anymore. Real connection requires being physically in the presence of one another, so it heightens the immediacy of consequence but also tests our willingness to be vulnerable. When we are physically close, other than running away from our actions, we see the results of what we do. We see others' reactions to us. But when the consequences aren't physically obvious, there is less impetus to change or learn. If there are no repercussions influencing your actions and no judgment to be fearful of, you will choose to act only in ways that benefit you or support your prejudices.

"Since when has the world of computer software design been about what people want? This is a simple question of evolution. The day is quickly coming when every knee will

bow down to a silicon fist, and you will all beg your binary gods for mercy."

—*Bill Gates*

Electronic communication provides convenience but lacks face-to-face non-verbal cues and behaviors that help us understand one another. We are only seeing a fraction of the message being conveyed, and that makes determining intent more difficult. In communicating electronically, we are becoming more and more dependent on symbols to communicate and even shortening words to a symbolic form to express ourselves with the least effort. In using emoji to convey our emotions, we are picking a symbol someone else designed to replicate how we feel. Your feelings are reduced to symbolism. No rebuttal, no discussion, no real understanding, and no guarantee that anyone is even looking or caring. We even have the capability now to manufacture a more flattering likeness of ourselves or turn our likeness into a cartoon as easily as choosing what we will wear. And that can't help but reinforce our dissatisfaction with ourselves as we are.

With the internet, a single individual's thoughts are multiplied exponentially throughout the world in the space of a moment, so we feel powerful, we feel heard, but there is no guarantee of being understood. And especially because of the anonymity of the user, the consequence of the message is deferred to all that view it.

"The real problem is not whether machines think but whether men do."

—*B.F. Skinner*

If you consider what has been said here about conscious thought and reading intentions, how is it even possible to know the intent behind the millions of minds trying to be "influencers"? The threats we face for the illusion of connectedness are like putting a bomb in the hands of a baby. We talk about the value of staying "connected" when in fact, we are increasingly disconnected from what actually grows, teaches, and emotionally sustains us. Virtual reality may eventually allow us to have experiences previously unavailable to us. Still, we need to remember that in a virtual world, we are dealing with a program, a human creation, or someone else's vision whose intent has populated the experience. We are interacting with a ghost of unknown origin. When we make 'choices' within a program, the programmer is the one who has decided where it takes us and has chosen the consequences. Kind of like a creator, right? But one that has no moral compass or divine wisdom to offer us.

Deciding where to place your trust is always a gamble. Anytime you are unable to rely on the truth of what you are told, you are choosing to be insecure. Rather than bringing us together, an anonymous environment allows us to be invisible. To feel safe in such a huge 'space,' we may align ourselves with groups and ideologies we believe will represent us. Your single voice is soon aligned with thousands. But who is controlling the narrative, and whose intent is being served? Most online organizations may have a set ideology that you can choose to represent you and your voice. But your voice just becomes a number supporting the intent of those controlling the organization. Do you feel heard now? Do you feel your voice has value?

There also is an inherent danger, especially for young people, of being exploited by an online community. Teenagers' intense desire for belonging and the strong influence of peer pressure combined with an anonymous platform is a dangerous combination. A virtual 'community' has no concern for an individual's well-being. A community that tells them what is attractive and what trends they should be involved in. A community that suffers no consequences for the damage that it causes. There are always those who will try to manipulate young people by assuming different identities and luring them off-line. The risks are huge when we open our front door and invite in the world, and we can carry that world in our hands. How can a child ever be equipped to deal with it?

> *"Technology is just a tool. In terms of getting the kids working together and motivating them, the teacher is the most important."*
>
> —*Bill Gates*

Only when we are physically near one another do we experience some level of risk, of being vulnerable, of experiencing real consequences. But we also know when we are heard, valued, and understood. That we are accepted as we are. That our voice is our own. All things that should never be lost or disvalued for the sake of convenience or entertainment.

> *"A mountain is composed of tiny grains of earth. The ocean is made up of tiny drops of water. Even so, life is but an endless series of little details, actions, speeches, and thoughts. And the consequences whether good or bad of even the least of them are far-reaching."*
>
> —*Swami Sivananda*

23 Truth and Relationships

There are relationships we choose and relationships that we have accepted through the choices we make. We commonly think of them as personal, but they can be business, service-related, or even our relationship to the environment. Relationships are where our emotional and spiritual work is done. Being physically present is always the hardest place to be truthful because we have opened ourselves to judgment. But there really isn't any risk in being truthful. We can only be hurt if we give others the power to hurt us in some way. If we aren't lying and being deceitful, we have no reason to hide. When we are at our best and most authentic, any judgment becomes meaningless and cannot hurt us. We can realize that others' judgment is just a misunderstanding. We can't be any more than what we are. If someone wants to judge us, that is on them, and we can just have compassion for their need to do so. It seems incongruent, but the hardest place to be truthful with your thoughts and feelings is usually with your family. Harder even than with a stranger. When you are with strangers, you can retreat and simply walk away. You can deny the judgment of those who do not know you. But it's harder to retreat from those closest to us; our lives are too intertwined, our histories and failures are known, and the consequences become more immediate and personal. Because our words routinely feed or starve one another's emotional security, we owe it to our spouses, children, parents, and ourselves to act with the best of intentions and be the best version of ourselves. Sharing what you discover about yourself with someone who loves you is the first step in maintaining a healthy relationship. Help them know you.

In reality, we are never really in control of the world around us. Judgment from strangers is a normal part of our interactions, you can't avoid it, but you do have control over how you feel about it. But judgment from those closest to us is the most damaging to our self-esteem. It's not as easy to brush off the attitudes of those who know us as those that don't. So, when we congratulate ourselves on not judging the people we meet, do we also consider how often we judge our loved ones? And is that judgment based upon our expectations, or are we silently intending disrespect?

When we lie, it seems to distance us from judgment and shelter us, at least temporarily. But lying denies any possibility of understanding and acceptance. You will continue to feel that who you are or what you have done is unworthy. If you feel the need to lie, you have already judged yourself badly. You aren't going to risk allowing the truth of your action to be known. But how someone judges you doesn't have to be a threat if you don't make it one. You can offer your truth and simply accept any responsibility there may be. But you must allow for the interaction to happen, the reaction to be there. You can even admit that you were being deceptive because you were afraid of failing or being judged and open the interaction to be better understood. Just your willingness to be truthful will give you a reason to feel good. It is freeing, not fear-inducing. When you allow yourself to share, you are not only trusting the other person, but you are trusting the truth to guide your life in a good way. Exchange your fear for faith. Extend your trust to others and be worthy of their trust in you as well.

When we share our thoughts and feelings, we are allowing ourselves to be vulnerable and creating an intimate space. We usually think of intimacy as physical closeness, but it can be emotional, intellectual, or spiritual. Moments can be intimate. Moments when you are confiding in a friend, when you are consoling a grieving family member, and especially when you are telling someone a truth that is difficult for you. Intimacy, in its truest sense, is about trust, being open to sharing something of ourselves, not to get or gain but simply to share.

So, we should get over having a purely sexual view of intimacy. We are more than our physical needs. We are missing out when we assume an attraction to someone must only be physical. We are denying ourselves the richness of relationships when we give ourselves away in casual physical encounters. Someone may be a teacher or help you to heal. People will be attracted to the sense of freedom and acceptance that you offer. There is no telling where an encounter may take you or what you can learn from it, however brief it may be. Accept the connections you make as opportunities. Think about them and feel what is there for you to do or to be. Those opportunities may also be a place or time, not necessarily a person. Look for guidance there. What is it telling you? It may be a sign that you are where you should be. Or maybe you are somewhere or with someone like you have been with before, and you're being given a chance to make a different kind of choice.

"The day the child realizes that all adults are imperfect, he becomes an adolescent; the day he forgives them, he becomes an adult; the day he forgives himself, he becomes wise."

—Alden Nowlan

To nurture your goodness, you should have people in your life that believe in you. But to foster those connections, you must be willing to let them in on who you are. Start by feeding your relationships some trust. Accept that where you are and who is there is a result of your choice. The consequence stands before you; learn from it! Their consequence is you; what can you give them? Perhaps the biggest gift we can give one another is our time and attention. Give it, don't rush it, or listen, only waiting for your chance to speak. Express your needs and fears but also share your journey. But make truth the anchor for your story. Listen for theirs.

"The reality of the other person lies not in what he reveals to you, but what he cannot reveal to you. Therefore, if you would understand him, listen not to what he says, but rather to what he does not say."

—*Kahlil Gibran*

Sharing takes courage. Being willing to trust takes courage. And each time we extend ourselves in those ways, we become stronger and more confident. We can stop giving others the power to restrict our expression when we stop taking their judgment to heart as true. Just eliminating the threat judgment represents to you will make you stronger emotionally.

"Any person capable of angering you becomes your master."

—*Epictetus*

24 Watch Out!

All of us have the ability to see things for what they really are, but most of the time, we choose not to. It feels good to play make-believe. We believe we are too smart to be taken in. It's normal to see things through a filter of desire. It gives us hope. But fantasies are bound by their nature to fail because there is no reality to them. We choose to see what we want. We dream of what others can provide for us. The nature of the con is in our gullibility to believe in whatever is offered, even in our jobs. We dream of what our profession can provide for us, not foreseeing what we will have to give up or how it will affect the quality of our life. We all want to base our choices on what we are told, but whether that is true always seems to be a gamble. So, you should always be wary of what promises to meet your needs and especially your desires. People don't offer promises unless that promise is a hook baited to meet their own needs. To really promise involves a personal commitment, and that isn't something done lightly.

There will always be individuals who seek to take advantage of or deceive you either as a reaction to their own pain or fear or to manipulate the situation in their favor. Some of those behaviors may have worked well for them for so long that they are deeply ingrained. So, until the consequences become devastating to their lives or they stop working, they have little reason to change. When they experience unpleasant consequences, they will see it as fate, bad luck, or someone else's fault and will quickly move on. Change for those who take advantage of others usually comes like lightning or not at all. It is too easy for them to cast blame when they are caught. The world becomes their adversary to outwit or deceive. But, in trying to control the world around them, they are causing their own suffering.

Our unmet needs and subconscious programming will seek out the very experiences that we need to heal from. We may invite past trauma into our lives over and over again, welcome it like an old friend. Like children of alcoholic parents who subconsciously seek out an alcoholic partner because it is such a familiar part of them. Or they invite those into their lives to try and fix them. It is normal for those who grew up with substance abuse around them to keep taking the blame that was put on them. In those relationships, you may actually enable your partner's destructive behaviors because you believe you can change them if you care enough. Then their demons become your failure. The change needs to be your own. Realize those kinds of attractions that draw you in so completely may be exactly what you need to heal from.

If you are looking for someone to rescue you or feel you must rescue others, that is a sure sign there are unresolved issues and unhealthy emotional needs that will turn your fairy tale into a soap opera. There is a big difference between rescue and support. It is natural to need love and to want acceptance. But it is also natural that those needs will bias you to accept easy fixes and empty promises. Your needs will be a lure attracting those who would seek to take advantage.

Expectations are a double-edged hook between people. Our expectations create a fantasy. Desire overwhelms reasonable thought, and most of us just follow along with what we feel or are led to believe. At this point, expectations, whether voiced or silent, bind us to each other. We want to feel needed and desired. But remember that expectations are a theft. Manipulation is violence. And there should be no expectation of any form of "payment" in a relationship. It shouldn't be, "I'll do this if you do that."

Falling in love is all feelings, feelings, feelings, and seldom thought! "Drunk" with infatuation and expectations, we may rush into relationships that barely survive the "sobering up." Romantic attraction is usually based upon a rush of hormones and subconscious needs. But what actually is the attraction? What is the "hook" that is drawing you in or drawing them to you? We like to believe it is physical beauty or physical prowess that is the core of attraction, but it goes much deeper than that. When we are attracted to something, it is a call on our awareness, a calling out of our need. We should not just heed the call of what attracts us but learn from it. But like the sirens of mythology that sound so sweet, look closely at what calls to you. In seduction, others are trying to control us. Defined, seduction is "to attract or lead someone away from proper behavior or thinking;" to persuade. Seduction's purpose is to mislead. Our egos don't automatically differentiate between attraction and seduction. We feel what we feel and believe what we want to believe, true or not.

"Anxiety [Fear] is love's greatest killer. It makes others feel as you might when a drowning man holds on to you. You want to save him, but you know he will strangle you with his panic."

—*Anaïs Nin*

We should not expect a relationship to solve our problems; it is irresponsible and damaging. Manipulating yourself into someone's life is dishonest and hurtful. We would not go to someone's home and bring our garbage with us; that would be disrespectful. But we may want to escape our problems by making them our partner's responsibility. Some relationships become just another quick fix for our emotional ills. We all know it takes time to get past the posing we do when we are dating. It takes time to earn someone's trust and love. Even considering that "love at first sight" is possible, that doesn't happen just because you want it to.

Think of your teenage years when you were not concerned with the effect you had on one another's lives and were only concerned with how you were perceived or what you could get. How many lives are irreparably changed during those years by inconsiderate actions and promises or decisions? How many adults still act that way? Love should not be an object, a word to manipulate someone, or a debt that is owed. You can't own love or demand it. But in attraction, it's all about the moment for once, how you feel, what you want, never a consideration for what is best. Our euphoria overwhelms even our subconscious mind. Compassion and friendship are healthy; infatuation is temporary insanity.

> *"In real love, you want the other person's good. In romantic love, you want the other person."*
>
> —Margaret Anderson

We've all seen controlling relationships. The entire basis of control is fear and insecurity. People seek control because they are afraid. Afraid of being discovered or judged in some way. Projecting that fear onto others, they need someone to control. Some may belittle and demean another's self-worth to build their own. They create insecurity in others, where they cast themselves as the protector. The only control they understand is the control they have over others, not themselves. Wanting to control someone is not healthy or loving; it is cowardly. Saying "I love you" does not make it so. If someone threatens to take their love and attention away, it wasn't there to begin with. To most of us, control seems physical, but most control is emotional. People are torn down mentally and carry the scars of that abuse for their entire lives. Watch out for those trying to exert control over you, and watch that you are not the one doing that either. We know right away when we are hurt emotionally, but how often do we consider how we may be hurting others? Only people that are hurting hurt others. Understand that. No matter if you are the one that was hurt or possibly hurting someone else, decide to stop the cycle and rise above what may have brought you there.

"If you are willing to look at another person's behavior toward you as a reflection of the state of their relationship with themselves rather than a statement about your value as a person, then you will over a period of time cease to react at all."

—Yogi Bhajan

"Love sees clearly, and seeing, loves on. But infatuation is blind; when it gains sight, it dies."

—Mary Roberts Rinehart

"Experience is not what happens to you – it's how you interpret what happens to you."

—Aldous Huxley

---

25   Blessing the Generations

> *"We cannot always build the future for our youth, but we can build our youth for the future."*
>
> —Franklin D. Roosevelt

I believe that there is nothing more important for the future than being a good parent and nothing more personally challenging. Our personal journey and how we treat our family will become the foundation of our children's emotional lives and affect the decisions made by them in the future.

> *"Each new generation is reared by its predecessor the latter must therefore improve in order to improve its successor. The movement is circular."*
>
> —Emile Durkheim

So, if you care about the health and happiness of future generations, this is where it begins. It's not someone else's job. It's not something that can be fixed later on. If you become a parent or caregiver, it is your job. Their future depends on you. You can help your children have loving, healthy relationships as adults by modeling those behaviors now. They will copy what they see every day, not just listen to what you say. Children don't get to choose their parents, but you have chosen to be one. Your choice may not have been deliberate, but remember that all your actions are a choice, and sadly much of the time, children may simply be a consequence of that choice. But whether having a child was intentional or not, it's vastly important to try and understand "what makes *you* tick" if you want your children to grow unburdened by your neurosis and addictions. Unfortunately, when we are in our childbearing years, we seldom have the energy or desire for self-reflection or change. Young adults, barely out of the nest, are out providing for their family's basic needs and finding their own way in the world. That is just the nature of things. Maturity doesn't come at a certain age and may still be a long way off for a lot of us. Historically, in tribal settings, the elders were tasked with raising the children. They had the time to devote to the children and the patience and wisdom to guide them. Those societies didn't expect children to raise children. It would have been seen as irresponsible. Children belonged to the tribe, not just the parents. Young adults took on the work needed in the community and continued to be mentored by the elders in their cultural ways and expectations. It's difficult even to perceive that way of life was possible, and yet it still exists in some cultures. It does illustrate that when it comes to raising our children, we should support one another by being present for any child, not just our own. I realize (as a parent myself) that it is difficult to trust others to be in our children's lives. But especially if we are personally experiencing difficult times and hard emotional issues, we should try to put our children ahead of ourselves. They don't have a choice. Instead of using your children as bargaining chips or confidants in our failed relationships, they need to be the top priority. If you deal with your struggles by only seeking to escape them or believing that finding the right partner will meet all your needs, that is what you are teaching them. We may not want to see ourselves as a detriment to our children's emotional health, but by acknowledging the role we play, perhaps we can embrace some change in ourselves for their sake. Like it or not, we are the model for their future relationships, so we need to set an example of living in a loving way.

We can give our children so much more than just a roof over their heads, food on the table, or a share in the wealth we've accumulated. Our time and compassion are vital to them and gifts that don't cost us anything. Even if your children now have children of their own, they are still learning from you. You are always teaching; either you are teaching them something valuable or teaching them something they will have to overcome. The term, teachable moments, can be taken to heart. No parent ever really knows if they are doing it "right." But you *can* model love and caring; you can always give that.

"Parents, deliberately or unaware, teach their children from birth how to behave, drink, feel, and perceive. Liberation from these influences is no easy matter."

—*Eric Berne*

Remember, it is not what you recite to your children that instills good values; it is what they see and hear. What they experience when they are young is what they will subconsciously imitate as they get older. If children see their parents fighting, that's what they learn, even though they may be punished for fighting themselves. If they don't see a healthy relationship between their parents, they will be unable to recognize what a healthy relationship is or how to handle frustration and anger in a constructive way. If you manipulate those around you to get what you want, that is how your child will act to get their own needs met. You can tell your child that lying is wrong, but if they see you laughing or benefiting from having deceived someone, they will associate lying and deception as a legitimate way to get their needs met. If you routinely judge others, your children will as well. If you seek to escape tough situations rather than facing them, that's how your children will cope when their lives get difficult. If you carry your prejudices around like a badge of honor, your children may adopt them as well and learn that hatred is expected of them.

"The surest way to corrupt a youth is to is to instruct him to hold in higher esteem those who think alike rather than those who think differently."

—Friedrich Nietzsche

If you look at your own childhood, it shouldn't be hard to see the consequences of your parents' decisions and behaviors on your life. You can begin to recognize where you learned to react the way you do. You can begin to appreciate how important your role as a parent is and the consequences for your children of the choices you make.

As adults, when we are in public, we expect to be held accountable for our behavior. Most of us care about how others see us or judge us, so we act in ways that we are expected to. But at home, we act as if the opinion of our family members doesn't matter, that our behavior toward them doesn't matter. We want to believe that our children are deaf, dumb, and blind to our ugly behavior. Unfortunately, as we aren't likely to be held accountable at home, we often don't treat our family with the same courtesy or respect that we do to total strangers. But we still expect our families to love us unconditionally no matter how we behave. "Do as I say, but not as I do." But truly, it is within our families that our character and compassion count the most. The complexity of family relationships provides the most fertile ground for learning how to love and speak the truth, but unfortunately, this closeness also provides ample opportunity for abuse. Even in the 'best' of situations, children are constantly under a blanket of judgment. Their self-esteem is directly tied to their performance in measuring up to adult expectations. Perhaps those expectations are set to keep them safe, instill values, or teach them skills to prepare them for life. But to a child, expectations, and judgment feel like failure, that they can never be good enough. Children may be told that they are loved but then treated cruelly. They will go forward in their lives not understanding what being loved truly feels like or how to love. As young parents, we parent as we experienced being parented. "That's how I was raised, and I turned out all right!" If you think that "all right" is good enough, then no amount of self-reflection will probably make a difference. Your own parents were only playing out what they learned from theirs. Casting blame doesn't change the past or the present, but you can change the future if you want to. You can decide for yourself what kind of parent you want to be. See yourself as a teacher to your child rather than a caretaker. That simple frame of mind can transform your relationship with them and, at the same time, help you come to terms with your own past.

It doesn't matter how good a person you portray yourself to be if you aren't even trying to be that for your family. Your true legacy will always be your behavior. Your children will learn to fear, learn to hate, or learn to love. Learn to escape from life's stresses or to overcome them.

"Children have never been very good at listening to their elders, but they have never failed to imitate them."

—James Baldwin

But how do we teach the importance of truth to our children? As parents, we should always model truth rather than the ease of deceit and avoidance. Let your child see you handle difficult choices in a healthy way. Let them see you consider how their decisions might affect others.

"Your kids require you most of all to love them for who they are, not to spend your whole time trying to correct them."

—Bill Ayers

Always encourage them to be truthful and acknowledge how brave they are when they tell the truth or share difficult things with you. Let them know you understand it isn't always easy. That easy isn't what we were put here for. That easy doesn't make us strong or grow us. Don't ever punish them for being truthful. Protect them, yes, but don't shield them completely from the world. Help them understand that their actions may not have been a good choice, but it does not make them a bad person. Help them identify and acknowledge how they are feeling. Teach them empathy and ask them to visualize how someone else might feel in a given situation. Teach them what loving actions are and what compassion is. Help them understand the consequences of harmful intentions and actions. Encourage them to personally address the harm they may have done by making what amends they can. And as was said before, help them understand there are some decisions that are life-changing ones.

Children need to learn how important choices are, how to weigh the options and consequences, and choose to do the right thing, rather than the easy thing or what makes them feel good for the moment. Ultimately, it isn't anyone's philosophy or theology that makes moral, compassionate adults; it is what children see practiced every day, especially between their parents.

> *"If there is anything that we wish to change in the child, we should first examine it and see whether it is not something that could better be changed in ourselves."*
>
> —*Carl Jung*

Love your children so they can recognize love, know how to love, and know they deserve it. Make sure that they know your love is not conditional. An old axiom states that you don't have to like your relatives all the time; you just have to love them. We are not perfect. We were never meant to be.

26 The World Around Us

As we learn about ourselves and what internal beliefs influence us, let's also consider the external influences that surround us and provide the fuel for our reactions.

We cannot choose where we are born any more than we can choose our parents. We are born into an economic, cultural, and political environment we did not choose, and to some extent, we inherit those values as well. Cultural norms are generally the first influences that teach us how to interact with each other.

The external world mirrors our internal human challenges. In projecting our fears, we create enemies; our greed poisons us, and our want creates lack. At one time, we identified ourselves with the geography and culture we came from. We were mountain people, river people, southerners, islanders, etc. Our behaviors and customs were designed around the environments we lived in. When those environments were damaged, it damaged us as well. But now, with the ease of travel and communication, we can just move. And even as we can interact globally and bring our cultures with us, we are no longer confined to a locale or even a country. But interacting globally, where there are such a wide array of influences vying for our attention, money, and faith, we may find it comforting to identify ourselves more intensely within our culture. We become more and more polarized in our attempt to carve out our identities from the mayhem. So rather than using this amazing opportunity to understand one another, communication has become less about sharing and being understood than competing with one another for influence. We want our way to be the right way. We can't stand the thought of being challenged for how we define ourselves. And the further we travel from what has defined us, the more we cling to it.

Just being born within our current economic system, advertising probably influences us more than our families do. With the corporate ownership and sponsorship of the media, marketing isn't confined to selling products and services but also ideas and opinions. Perception managers create messages to change our views to a desired perspective. As a holdover from the past, we are encouraged to believe that if it is reported in the media, it must be true. But, in the recent past, the court actually ruled that news organizations do not have to report truthfully. So, the news that is reported doesn't have to be true or even be news. Information is power and is used or withheld on the whims of commerce and politics. Corporate law allows individuals to be shielded from the consequences of poor products and services. Success in business and politics seems to favor the better liars or those with enough money to buy your vote. You may reason that your vote hasn't been paid for, but big money goes into manipulating your opinion and stoking up your fear.

With the infinite amount of information that confronts us every day, we subconsciously filter out most of what we hear. But that doesn't mean it won't find a place in your mind. We do not have the time or energy to sort out every truth or falsehood. The bombardment of information and the lack of accountability have contributed to our indifference. But even if we can numb ourselves to all the 'junk mail' influences that come our way, if you are aware of something, you cannot help but be influenced by it. Influenced without the benefit of knowing the truth of the message or the intent of the sponsor.

Consider the true intent of advertising. Advertising is not produced to give you relevant information but to make a profit regardless of your welfare. Simply realizing the incredible amount of money and resources it takes to advertise to you gives you an indication of the number of money businesses and politicians stand to gain. And market forces are counting on the fact that any message repeated often enough will be regarded as true.

On a more personal level, you may be challenged to have one set of ethics at home and another at work. Your employer may require you to make certain decisions under the assurance that it's "just business." That your behavior, decisions, and consequences are hidden safely behind the corporate structure. Our need to be employed and provide for our families may limit our choices, but you can always bring some integrity to anything you labor at. You can bring your values with you each day and perhaps influence the decisions that are made. Think of all the ways being hidden allow us to be irresponsible. A politician may place a vote that culminates in the death of thousands but claims to represent family values. When we aren't held personally responsible for our decisions, we tend to focus only on our personal gain and consequently wind up acting inhumanely.

"Society has gotten to the point where everybody has a right but nobody has a responsibility."

—*Unknown*

When our society turns away from the value of truth, it leaves us standing on shifting sands. We feel powerless and uncertain because we know down deep that we cannot trust the information given to us. Our gut may tell us something is wrong. We lose faith in our institutions to protect us. We buy into the lie that we are powerless to change anything. Even those realizations are used against us, using our tendency to blame to create division in our communities and pit us against each other. We go along to get along, because we are routinely denied choices or given so many choices it has short-circuited our desire to discern good ones. But we *can* counter the effects of our modern world by standing up for something as simple and revolutionary as telling the truth to each other. Having compassion and standing for things that benefit the needs of people, not the greed of individuals.

Truth may seem insignificant to some, but it really is essential. We may feel that lying holds change at bay, and it may for a time. But movement is inevitable; change always occurs. Consequences are building. Nothing is more powerful than the truth, and it cannot be denied or ignored. The truth wants nothing but to be. And it's simple; let's just challenge ourselves to tell just one truth and reject one excuse at a time. Accept change as movement that is necessary. Think, feel, and act larger than where you find yourself.

"The only way to deal with an unfree world is to become so absolutely free that your very existence is an act of rebellion."

—Albert Camus

---

27 Empowerment

"Truth becomes as conqueror only to those who have lost the art of receiving it as friend."

—Rabindranath Tagore

Empowerment is the ability to independently make choices relevant to one's situation. Conscious choices are born out of considered thought, not emotional reactions. When you react emotionally, you are acting out of response to another's intent, not your own, and you are giving away your power to decide. You are powerful when you can stand behind your decisions and are willing to accept the consequences. To consciously accept where you are and how you arrived there gives you the ability to get where you want to be. The "where you want to be" can be an emotional, physical, or even financial place. Empowerment isn't something you need to have bestowed on you. You always have the ability to be in control of your life and your decisions. Perhaps you aren't exactly where you'd like to be, but you always have power over how you react to it. How you feel is up to you. If you decide to be tired and defeated, that is what you will be. If it is too overwhelming, ask for guidance, and go forward in faith rather than fear. To conquer your fears, realize that nothing of true value can be taken from you. Fear doesn't gain you anything, not even protection, not sympathy, not healing. Material possessions may come and go, but your freedom to think and reason and your sense of self can never be taken away. The greatest power you have is the power of your mind and your heart. That power can only be lost if you voluntarily relinquish it.

If your dishonesty arises out of fear, then emotional security rises from truth. In understanding what you are afraid of or simply recognizing that you are afraid, you can then just choose to be brave. When you know that your reaction is a choice, then know also that you have the ability to make a different one. Empowered by that knowledge, you will be able to face much more than you can imagine. You are stronger than you think. There is nothing that can control you, not even your fear. In fearing anything, you are giving power to what you are reacting to. Turn that power inward instead, consciously limit your reaction, or don't react at all; you *don't have to*.

Every time we lie or make excuses to protect ourselves, we can never know the whole cost or consequence of doing so. We believe that by placing blame, we are transferring that consequence. We feel like when we lie, we are in control. But we have lost control. Your intent may be invisible, but it is behind all your actions, and the consequences will be visible to all. No matter how powerful you believe yourself to be, you cannot hide from the spiritual effects of what you do. But you can enhance the spiritual nature of your actions by speaking truthfully and making those actions compassionate ones. Truth is empowering; make it a friend instead of a servant to your needs or an adversary. Truth bequeaths power, and it is truly the only thing that does empower you.

You give your power away when you rely on others. But it seems so much easier to trust someone than to understand a situation or do it for yourself. We spend a lot of energy hoping where we place our trust is warranted. When you empower someone to decide for you, you are literally loaning out your trust. So, when you do trust, don't be a slave to it. Give it and let it go so you do not give your well-being away with it. Give your trust freely without expectation by being willing to own the consequence if your trust is betrayed. Don't curse those who betray it. You chose to give it. When you let your trust out into the world, you don't own it anymore; what you do own is your reaction to the result.

All you can do is try and know something about the person or organization you are trusting and realize that everything can and will change, so expect it to! But don't set yourself up to be deceived or disappointed by holding on so tightly to how things are that any change is painful for you.

"We are never so vulnerable than when we trust someone – but paradoxically, if we cannot trust, neither can we find love or joy."

—Walter Anderson

At a societal level, during times of the greatest instability and economic uncertainty, there is also the most fraud and bigotry. There are people and institutions waiting in place to provide you with easy answers and put you in a box they can control or define to their benefit. Stepping into line for some promise of security provides only insecurity. Joining a group physically or mentally satisfies your insecurity because you place your faith in the fact that others are doing it as well. You delegate your will to the group. But when you give up finding your own answers, you will ride the tide of consequence along with everyone else. I know it's difficult to know all we should in this day and age. But we can be selective in whom we trust and delegate our decision-making carefully. Don't believe that the world has become too complicated to know what is right for you. Choose what you are able to know about. Don't think, because the choices seem endless, that your decisions are endless as well.

"You may not control all events that happen to you, but you can decide not to be reduced by them."

—Maya Angelou

28 Thought and Prayer

The concepts of thought and prayer are, by their nature, esoteric. ("A knowledge of things not easily grasped by the intellect alone...") But if those concepts are not easily grasped, conceptualizing thought *being* prayer would likely take considerable effort and study. But perhaps not so much. We are all thinking beings. We know what it is to have thoughts. We all experience need, desire guidance, and probably have a belief in something greater than "ourselves." Perhaps then it is easy to understand that prayer is not just reciting pious words or petitioning the Creator for our needs but actually placing our focus (thoughts) on what is going on within us. Do you really believe that an all-powerful, all-seeing Being is unable to know what is in your heart unless you speak it? Or is prayer more an opportunity for *you* to discover what is deep within your heart, and the act of voicing it or offering it up to what you have faith in fixes it firmly in your mind? Prayer, then, is simply what is real and true within you at that moment. We don't feel the need to lie when we are in prayer. You may feel shame or fear the consequences of your behaviors, but when in prayer, we aren't being judged or inadequate. But believe in the mercy and grace of the Creator (however you believe). When you pray, you begin reducing the noise of your mind to focus on what your intention is. Your emotions, especially when they seem overwhelming, are a gift, a way to experience your need and to release it. When you cry, it is a prayer; when you laugh, it is as well. When you feel grief, that is a prayer, a connection to the love you felt. All comes from the heart, not the mind. When we shift away from thinking, feeling is all we have left, and we are touching the truth of ourselves. But the minute we try and use words to vocalize our feelings, we drift away from our heart into our mind, which only reaffirms our separateness.

When you are talking, you can't hear. When you are composing words in your mind, you aren't listening. When you get silent, you can be guided. Our thought processes have been called an internal dialogue. Your internal *conscious* dialogue is more than just a conversation with yourself. When you are thinking consciously, you are connecting yourself purposely to what is confronting you. You are activating your intent. And if your intent reflects your need, it is prayer; it is seeking, even if it doesn't sound like you have been taught prayer to be. But if your intent is to deceive, you have left the Creator out of the picture and have moved your life away from what sustains you.

"The mind of the individual seeking help is the Christ-mind—awaiting recognition."

—*Joel Goldsmith*

Truth is more than just a concept; it *lives* within us. Those beautiful words of devotion we have come to accept as prayer may help quiet our busy mind like spiritual-sounding words that give us a vocabulary for that experience. But the most truthful prayers are simply our tears, our fears, our gratitude, or a simple conversation with the Creator that says, "I am hurting and need your help." Prayers should be said not to get or gain but to heartfully share our human frailty. And it shouldn't be confined to houses of worship or only when we are in a quiet space. Those are all ways we may use to initiate our focus but aren't necessary. To pray ceaselessly is to be in conversation with God about what is true for us each moment, intending to be in a prayerful space wherever that may be. But to return to the beginning, if thoughts *are* prayer and you take that to heart, would you begin to think differently? When you experience strong emotions, will you accept the message they are sending you?

"Whether we realize it or not, prayer is the encounter of God's thirst with ours. God thirsts that we may thirst for him."

—St. Augustine

"True prayer is neither a mere mental exercise nor a vocal performance. It is far deeper than that. It is a spiritual transaction with the creator of Heaven and Earth."

—Charles Spurgeon

"Let us have no addresses to which God's grace is to be sent because God is not interested in one person more than in another."

—Joel Goldsmith

---

29 Miracles

> "To define a miracle as a violation or suspension or overriding of natural laws is already to presuppose what nature is like. It is also to impose prior limits on divine action."
>
> —William Dembski

Most of us believe that miracles only appear or are possible for the devoted and deserving few. When we hear the word "miracle," we think of otherworldly power, of unexplainable healings of fatal diseases or crippled bodies, of impending disaster averted, anything that seems beyond human capacity to control. But aren't even the simplest answers to our prayers and needs a miracle? When we consider these experiences fate or luck, we are diminishing and dismissing the wonder of miracles in our lives.

> "Luck is a word devoid of sense. Nothing can exist without a cause."
>
> —Voltaire

> "Miracles are a retelling in small letters of the very same story which is written across the whole world in letters too large for some of us to see."
>
> —C.S. Lewis

Miracles happen every day, all around us. It may be routine as an adult to accept most things as scientifically explainable but think of a child witnessing something they haven't seen before. Aren't the things we take for granted miracles to them? Faith becomes the vessel by which we experience and accept what we never understood before. Perhaps we imagine angels, bright lights, and prayerful hymns making the "impossible" happen. But here we are surrounded by the true spiritual nature of the world, and what we call miracles are cracks in our belief of how things are, where the reality of the divine shines through.

If we can be like children, with wide-eyed wonder and anticipation of what each moment might bring, life will open its pages, its text illuminated. You can learn to appreciate the series of miracles that is your life.

"It is the childlike mind that finds the kingdom."

—*Charles Fillmore*

"The Miracles of the Church seem to me to rest not so much upon faces or voices or healing power coming suddenly near to us from afar off, but upon our perceptions being made finer, so that for a moment our eyes can see and our ears can hear what is there about us always."

—*Willa Cather*

"In the presence of the God-realized, the laws of the material world do not apply. That's why people who live steadfastly at a place of God-consciousness can perform miracles."

—*Joel Goldsmith*

Our moments are sent to us by the Creator. He goes ahead of us and "makes the way." He knows where we will be ahead of our own thoughts and sends us what we need. Sometimes answers take some time to come. Or maybe they arrive quickly but go unnoticed. They may not come announced with neon lights to help us find them. We may walk right by, unaware of what we have passed because the answer doesn't take the form we imagine or wish for.

We may believe that miracles happen only in the presence of prayer, but if our thoughts are prayers, then miracles must be possible every moment. Everything is divine. Every decision is open to guidance, but we always have the free will to decide what we do or what we believe. So, what guides us when we decide to turn right or left, speak to someone, or walk by, offer help, or deny it? A single mother, out of money to feed her children, has needs that are obvious; she walks her prayer in her suffering. But what decision guides her to the place where she finds a 20-dollar bill on the ground or meets a stranger that can offer the help she needs? What series of circumstances caused the money to fall from someone's hand or wallet or have the extra money to offer help? Which of the events that led up to that prayer's answer was "the miracle" to that mother?

There may be a lot of time that passes before our prayers bear fruit, but there is no waiting that does not serve a purpose. Many things must be present to move the world to a place where all are blessed; all needs met, to move you to where your answers may be found. But it is up to you to recognize it, to accept being guided, to be moved to it. Not necessarily physically moved but moved in your understanding and willingness. Perhaps you just need more time to be ready. It isn't about whether you are worthy or not. We are all worthy of grace and healing. You will be given an infinite number of opportunities to get it right for as long as you live. Healing serves a purpose, and when we begin healing serves a purpose. Whom we choose to have help us has a purpose. The purpose is always greater than ourselves and what we need. But we must choose to be there, to show up. Healing of body, mind, and spirit together makes us understand our wholeness. The Creator sees us as we were created and doesn't perceive the infirmities, diseases, or weaknesses we believe in. In the divine presence, we are not judged or found wanting. We leave all the 'human conditions' behind when we leave this place. We always go back to being whole because that is what is true.

Those big "front page news miracles" are when the lie of our separateness from God has been stripped away, and in that unexplainable moment, truth is letting us glimpse our true human inheritance. But the little everyday miracles are no less miraculous. Think of the miracle of life itself, of a flower blooming, of a baby being born. Are they really without meaning?

"Miracles are a retelling in small letters of the very same story which is written across the whole world in letters too large for some of us to see."

—*C.S. Lewis*

---

30 What is Spirituality?

Many would define religion as a belief in the Creator. And most that participate in organized religious services wouldn't hesitate to define themselves as not just religious but spiritual people. But for people not historically part of organized religion, especially those who have been judged and persecuted for their beliefs, religion is something entirely different from just a belief in the Creator. With that in mind, consider that religion could also be defined as a social organization: an organization set up to provide a standardized interpretation of the original revelations that began it.

But for the individual, considering yourself to be a religious person or belonging to a specific faith isn't a prerequisite for being a spiritual person. Religious participation doesn't stop you from searching for your own spiritual nature. Belief isn't humanly created or led. But most people want to follow a leader that reassures them that they are attending to their spiritual needs through their participation in religious activity. Religions were created as an authority over a set of beliefs. Those looking for answers outside of themselves are drawn to where they think they will find them, and organized religion provides a socially acceptable avenue for spiritual study. But religious leaders only have to self-declare themselves as spiritually worthy to minister to others. And many use their religious authority to promote themselves and their dogma to their own advantage. So, we should be cautioned against accepting any authority as absolute, especially if those in authority promote distrust of ideas that challenge their teachings or try to politically influence their congregation through their biased interpretation of religious tenets.

> "A religion is a unified system of beliefs and practices relative to sacred things, that is to say, things set apart and forbidden—beliefs and practices which unite into one single moral community called a church, all those who adhere to them."
>
> —Emile Durkheim

Defined: Spirituality involves the recognition of a feeling or sense or belief that there is something greater than ourselves, something more to being human than sensory experience and that the greater whole of which we are part is cosmic or divine in nature.

Spirituality will always be a solitary experience; it is seeking a personal relationship with the Creator and trusting that through that relationship, divine guidance can be realized. Because of the solitary nature of that search, that relationship is uniquely different for each one of us. We should never judge how someone may be called or the quality of their experience or insist that one way is the only way. It is not necessary to be accepted or understood. Divine guidance is within and around us all. And in all forms and faiths. And within that guidance is an awareness of the true nature of the world and of us.

> "Enlightened leadership is spiritual if we understand spirituality not as some kind of religious dogma or ideology but as the domain of awareness where we experience values like truth, goodness, beauty, love, and compassion, and also intuition, creativity, insight, and focused attention."
>
> —Deepak Chopra

> "Spirituality is not a formula; it is not a test. It is a relationship. Spirituality is not about competency; it is about

intimacy. Spirituality is not about perfection; it is about connection. The way of the spiritual life begins where we are now in the mess of our lives."

—*Mike Yaconelli*

---

31 How Truth Will Change You

Truth gives you a firm foundation for your choices and actions and is the starting point on your journey of self-discovery. The you that you are seeking isn't found in what you want it to be or what you have been taught to believe by others' opinions. When you are truthful with yourself and let go of your fantasies, expectations, and even some of your fears, you will begin to understand your needs and where your reactions are coming from. You can let go of your dependence on others and can free yourself from their expectations and judgment.

When others can trust you to be truthful with them, they know they can trust their decisions regarding you. You are giving them security instead of doubt. Respect instead of deceit. When you know yourself and are confronted with a situation, you know you don't need to rush headlong to react. Even if it is happiness or joy, even if what you feel is fear or anger, you can use those feelings to understand the truth about yourself. You can see that how you feel can be a choice. You will soon realize the big difference between what you want to be true and what is true. Truth begins to move you mentally and physically in ways that benefit all those around you. Making a commitment to the truth, you won't be able to feign innocence of your actions anymore, nor would you want to. Consequences will be your teacher instead of an adversary. Truth will help you see how alike we all are and how afraid we all are, and you will be more compassionate and more willing to help. When you speak the truth and are willing to monitor your intentions, you gain a new perspective; create a new lens through which to see the world. Not a rose-colored lens that just pretties things up, but an entirely new prescription that makes things clear. That clarity super-charged with your compassion will wake you to the true essence of the world around you and your responsibility to it. When you take up the challenge to live truthfully and decide things consciously, you are a human *being*, not just being human.

But why should you make an effort? Why is it important? You should want to be a better human being because it is ingrained in us to do so. You will flow with the energies of life instead of fighting your way upstream, perhaps because you want to be a better person, parent, lover, or partner. Maybe you have had hard times in your life and want something better. But your own personal reasons aside, it's the right thing to do. The "Golden Rule" isn't an antiquated set of principles; it was something that, historically, we all agreed was of value because it worked and many have held these values as an integral part of a successful society.

"Just as you want others to do for you, do the same for them."

—*Luke 6:31*

"None of you [truly] believes until he wishes for his brother what he wishes for himself."

—*Muhammad*

"All things are our relatives; what we do to everything, we do to ourselves. All is really One."

—*Black Elk*

"The heart of the person before you is a mirror. See there your own form."

—*Socrates*

The truth about ourselves is that we are beings made up of emotional, physical, and spiritual parts. We react to our emotional experiences the same way as we do our physical experiences. When we touch a hot pan, we let go because we experience it burning us. We also know that hot pan could burn others, so we warn them or remove the threat. We are not afraid of the pan; we understand the consequence of touching it when it is hot. When we experience emotional pain, it is instinctual to try and avoid those situations. But not unlike being burned, any pain is a signal to protect us from further damage. What we take from those experiences is our choice. You can merely react, recoil, and do your best to avoid pain, or you can understand that certain situations require conscious thought and perhaps different decisions. Use those emotional moments as a vehicle to understand what you need to face. Because only when you understand where that pain and fear comes from will you actually be protecting yourself. You can see and change the choices that put you there. It is all too common to medicate away emotional discomfort and painful experiences. We have accepted the painful parts of life as a given to either suffer through or escape. But continual avoidance may ultimately keep you from healthy relationships. Back to the example: only understanding what heats the pan can inform you when not to touch it. Seeking the truth of yourself turns off the hot stove. There is no longer a need for relief or even a potholder! Truth can do that for you.

When you tell the truth, especially when you ache to hide in a lie, you have just conquered a great challenge. Feel good about it! Taking that emotional risk makes it easier to put those situations in the proper perspective. No matter how "successful" you may be, we all lie because we are afraid of being judged or rejected in some way. You will find that the more often you choose to be truthful, the harder it will be to lie. Your dishonesty will nag at you, eat away at your peace, and demand you come back into balance. You will know how corrupt lying is to you. You may initially think the "costs" of being truthful are too great, but you will find that truth is free and freeing.

"And as we let our own light shine, we unconsciously give other people permission to do the same. As we are liberated from our fear, our presence automatically liberates others."
—*Marianne Williamson*

You don't have to announce your truthfulness; it can be your secret. Your path will be self-evident to all around you. Suddenly, people will begin to seek you out and ask your advice because they seek some of the peace that you seem to have found. Some relationships may fall away as the dynamics of the interactions that brought you together begin to lose their power. It is sad and confusing when that happens, you may want that person to share your journey, but that will mean picking up their own, and they may not be ready to do so.

Relationships and community are nurturing, and you'll find that living this kind of life, your spiritual community will find you. Sharing with those also on this journey feels like coming home. But look for guidance before sharing what you have found and who you share it with. You may easily recognize the searching and need in others and want to help (and this may be what attracts them to you) but sharing with those who aren't ready to hear it will only disvalue your experience, as they will only see you as a threat to their understanding.

"If you can't even be a nice person, then forget about enlightenment."
—*Khen Rimpoche Tsewang Gyatso*

The path that was set out for you is not the only way. Every path leads to God. So, it's enough to step silently and invisibly with your prayer and simply pray that others' journeys are gentle ones. The Creator's timing is always perfect in what is brought to you or where you are led. Truth should teach you to embrace faith, not doubt it. Remember your prayers so you will recognize the answers when they come. Don't assume that your prayer or need will be answered only in the way you envision it because the time spent waiting may lead you to where you may answer to another's need as well. We *are* all connected.

"'Your task... to build a better world,' God said. I answered, 'How?... this world is such a large, vast place, and there's nothing I can do.' But God in all His wisdom said, 'Just build a better you.'"

—*Unknown*

Be thankful for the trials in your life. Trials are not there to punish us, and if we believe they are, we will avoid them. The consequences that test us teach us. Perhaps the difficulties that come your way are just a personal invitation to bring you back to prayer. We are always being guided and moved. The choices you make work with what you are called to or work against it. You cannot know how you are being molded and how the changes that you are going through will provide for you in the future. It is not the continued good in our lives that prompts our growth but the trials we suffer through. But that we suffer is our choosing. Living with a mindful appreciation of the inherent *God-ness* of the moment gives you the guidance you seek. It bears repeating that there is no good and bad in God; there is only God. *"I am what I am."* As you try to live consciously and seek what is true within you, ever so silently, changes will happen around you and to you, moving you into balance and using you to answer the needs of others. Acceptance, even in the face of suffering, strengthens you mentally; running from the slightest discomfort makes you weak. Facing discomfort, you learn endurance; turning your suffering over to God, you realize you are not alone. You don't need to run away; you don't need to hide in lies or self-denial; you never did. God speaks to us in everything surrounding us, but His voice is very quiet. He speaks to us in the love of our families, in the begging of the destitute, in the sharing of hard times, in the movement of the rivers, the weave of a spider's web; God's love is in the intake of our breath. Thoughts that arise within us, if there is truth in them, are prayers. If we choose to be positive and loving, that will be what our life becomes.

"God is closer than our hands and feet, closer than our breathing."

—Joel Goldsmith

"Mankind has always been but one humanity. We still are. It may even be prophesied that we probably always will be. Our great problem is and has been for ages, how to live with each other, with our fellow human beings. Religion in its core is what Jesus and Buddha and Lao Tzu and all the other sages have declared it to be: loving one another."

—Kenneth Patton

Truth is changing the world. This life we share is not broken into pieces; it is whole, and what each of us does touches us all.

"The events in our lives happen in a sequence in time, but in their significance to ourselves they find their own order the continuous thread of revelation."

—*Eudora Welty*

32   The Spiritual Challenge

Being truthful places us in a state of grace (divine favor) independent of religious dogma. Grace is not a reward but an uncovering of our inheritance. Regardless of whether we feel worthy or not, when we remain humble, we are already accepting divine guidance. It isn't necessary to adhere to any doctrine or belong to any religious group to be worthy of the blessings that truth brings to our lives. The most important truth is a spiritual one, and you make your way closer to it each time you choose truth over deceit or denial.

Historically, individuals would isolate themselves from society for long periods of time to gain spiritual awareness. They would avoid calling any attention to themselves as they sought only to be hollow bones for the Creator to animate. Even now, there are always some, but probably unrecognized. Being recognized is not their function. What enlightenment they attain, they attain for all of us. In general, any truly enlightened individuals will shun attention or the trappings of importance as those things are a detriment to their spiritual practice. Anyone achieving that level of self-mastery would be the first to say they are just a servant, nothing more, less than those they serve. Any accolades, followers, or material gifts only tie us to our egos and present tests which need to be overcome. It is good to appreciate and respect our teachers, healers, and elders, but show your gratitude by doing the work. Allow them their fidelity to the commitment they have made. Don't make a show of yourself and try to gain favor. Or expect to use their mind to find your own. Give them the gift of your time, unburdened by schedules and expectations. There are few that even consider commitment to a spiritual life a realistic calling, but unfortunately, to begin, many of those will be the first in line to latch onto anyone they believe can give them the answers. Many churchgoers may attend prayer groups or services, study religious texts, and attend services content in their beliefs and the guidance they are provided. Perhaps trying to be a good Christian, Muslim, Jew, Protestant, Islamist, or religious person of any culture is enough. But be counseled that religion in itself is not an answer, not a calling. And there is no true spiritual justification for any dogma that instructs you to vilify, judge, or condemn one another. There is no acceptable justification for hatred, judgment, or exclusion.

The most basic spiritual challenge is the challenge to "walk your talk" and take your values to heart in *all* you do, especially toward others. Personal growth won't happen unless you are willing to do the dirty work of dealing with your hatred, prejudice, and fears and trade them for a willingness to understand. A willingness to admit you are wrong for exacting revenge on others for your fears. It's always just been a choice. You can just choose not to do it.

We are the only part of creation that is self-aware. Other creatures may be sentient and are able to feel and react to what is around them. Some even experience emotions and carry their memories. But they carry no internal ethical conflicts around their behaviors. The awareness that we are experiencing an emotion and are responsible for our actions is uniquely human. Within your awareness, you instinctively know that there are parts to you that are not physical. There is more to life than most realize, just as you are more than the skin color, the size of your feet, or the color of your hair. The whys of our uniqueness and the where or for what purpose we are being guided are the "big questions" of human existence. Perhaps those big questions are the carrot and stick that draw us to a spiritual life where those answers may be found. But be prepared; once you engage in this journey, what comes to you may challenge what you have become comfortable believing and test your resolve to continue further, but there is no turning back. You can't unsee what you have seen or understood. Consciously or not, the spiritual dimension of us is intertwined with all that we do. Regardless of whether or not you have a religious affiliation, you have a personal relationship with the Creator. You tend to that relationship like any other in what you do and don't do. Being truthful and acting consciously and with compassionate intent, we keep the temple floors clean; we prepare for the understanding that will come when we do the work that is asked of us. When we align our body, mind, and spirit, we can be a hollow bone for the Creator to work through us. From that outpouring and giving of ourselves, we are also blessed many times over.

"I saw the angel in the marble and carved until I set him free."

—Michelangelo

Just the reading of spiritual truths does not bring them to life. Your mind must be ready; when it is, then understanding will blossom for you. Spiritual revelations are sparks that can start many fires. Fires that will continue to smolder and change over time through the filter of your experiences. We all have the ability to experience revelation; we don't need training to receive it, only an openness to it. You may share your experience, but no one can decipher it for you because it is not theirs. It is a private conversation meant for you alone.

"Information may inform the mind, but revelation sets a heart on fire."

—Matt Redman

> *"Prayer is the means by which men communicate with God. Revelation is the means by which God communicates with men."*
>
> —Marion G. Romney

If, as some believe, we are created in His image, then we are inheritors of all the health, wealth, love, and compassion that we define in that image. We come into this world perfect, even with our differences and disabilities, all still close to God. As we walk upon this earth, we can lift each other up when we recognize that is true for us and everyone we meet. The challenge is to walk that truth out into the world. Knowing that truth with all certainty, you help release your neighbor and all around you, at least temporarily, from their suffering until their personal cycle of choice begins again. Because it is always our choice. When we choose to be compassionate and allow ourselves to be guided, we become willing partners in the God-ness of the world. Noticing the synchronicities and coincidences that begin happening around you is a sign of your increasing enlightenment. You are becoming more in tune with the guidance you seek and are being led to where you should be. And all along the way, you are bringing with you the potential of the divine truth.

> *"According to Vedanta, there are only two symptoms of enlightenment, just two indications that a transformation is taking place within you toward a higher consciousness. The first symptom is that you stop worrying. Things don't bother you anymore. You become light-hearted and full of joy. The second symptom is that you encounter more and more meaningful coincidences in your life, more and more synchronicities. And this accelerates to the point where you actually experience the miraculous."*
>
> —Deepak Chopra

The Spiritual Challenge

"Our self-realization is the greatest gift we can give the world."

—Ramana Maharshi

33   Turning on the Light

All the understanding we seek is not out there somewhere. Truly everything we need is within us. The love we all need travels with us. We can struggle intellectually to understand, read, meditate, and take all the classes available to us and perhaps still only grasp a tiny taste of it. But when you put your questions out into the universe, bits and pieces of understanding, perhaps even revelation, will slowly rise to the surface out of that desire. Understanding comes in waves; the ebb and flow are not predictable or regular. Sometimes the water is still, other times turbulent, sometimes muddied, or clear. You will have awesome moments that will fill you till you think you have glimpsed the whole truth of the world, only to find your wonder fading over time. It may happen again and again, not at all, or perhaps only after a very long time. Your desire and eagerness don't equal readiness. And your readiness has nothing to do with being worthy or having the ability to understand but with doing the internal work necessary to clear the way for what is coming. You need to make a space for it. You will look back on the times of your most perfect understanding and realize how little you actually knew. And the same will be true later of what you know now. We will never be know-it-alls. We were never created to be. Understanding is a journey that has no end but endless rewards.

"… Approach the heart of the Buddha in the realm of absolute truth, and the Buddha will be there with you… You don't have to die to enter nirvana or the Kingdom of

God. You only have to dwell deeply in the present moment, right now."

—*Thich Nhat Hanh*

You get ready by walking your prayer. You walk your prayer in part by recognizing the intentions you put into the world, the choices you make, and the needs that drive you. You get ready by listening, connecting with yourself in silence, thinking, and questioning what moves you and why you react the way you do. It's important to recognize that all life is related, interdependent, and sacred, and what we do to any part of it, we do to ourselves. We need to be respectful of the generations by caring for the young and old. And listen for the voices that call out for our compassion and help. Make the choice to live with faith in the power and guidance of the Creator. In these ways, we eliminate our resistance and practice the qualities of our spiritual inheritance. When we stop trying to keep up with the world around us, we are more easily guided to where the answer is found. Remember, your subconscious mind only processes your past to protect your future. Neither the past nor the future are real. Only the present moment is real. Your subconscious conversations with yourself that cause you to react are just "an arm of the flesh" and not who you truly are.

"You are not your mind."

—*Eckhart Toile*

"As much complexity as there is to the known physical universe, from the atomic level and beyond to the enormity of the stars, there is the same within the spiritual world."

—*My Friend*

> *"Whatever is happening is the path to enlightenment."*
> —*Pema Chodron*

We have forgotten that we are the ones who decided to place God outside of ourselves and far away. That has been our choice. In believing in that separateness, we give power and life to disease, misery, and suffering. Your beliefs and fears are unnecessary armor you have used to protect yourself. Spiritually, we are not infirm, evil, disfigured, or unworthy. If you see someone as that, you are believing in a lie. The "kingdom" we aspire to doesn't include fear, prejudice, hate, injustice, illness, or even death. Those are part of the separateness we have come to accept. We get carried through life by the world around us and human reasoning. But that reasoning can also be applied to truth so that we can step outside of that physical world and into the spiritual one. Go back inside God's love and remember your true home.

> *"God is seated in the hearts of all."*
> —*Bhagavad Gita*

That it is our home is the only truth, and that truth heals all it touches when it is unveiled. I finally set this effort free. What it does out in the world and within you is in God's hands. Personally, I hope these ideas will lead you to think more consciously, more deliberately and especially more lovingly. As a servant it is my job to get out of the way but my intention was to sweep the path clearer for you. Our striving and searching alone are evidence that the kingdom exists. The challenge is to embrace the journey.

> *"The man of self-knowledge transcends life and death and lives in the ecstasy of divine consciousness."*
> —Shiva Negi

> *"Neither shall they say Lo here! Or, lo there! For behold, the kingdom of God is within you"*
> —Luke 17:21

> *"The highest revelation is that God is in every man."*
> —Ralph Waldo Emerson

The realization of our true nature makes us servants, not rulers. You may strive to be a hollow bone, through which blessings may manifest. But you can't do that unless you get our needs, desires, and intentions out of the way. The movement of that truth cannot be manipulated or used without consequence. That highest of revelations bestows on us the responsibility to arrive in the moment just a hollow bone. No meat, no marrow, but with tremendous joy.

To the Reader:
I invite your comments and inquiries! Please feel free to share with me at:

www.Challengeoftruth.com

www.ingramcontent.com/pod-product-compliance
Lightning Source LLC
Chambersburg PA
CBHW071348080526
44587CB00017B/3019